THE ART OF LETTING GO

THE ART OF LETTING GO

Free yourself and develop your inner strength

BY

KURT GASSNER

The Art of Letting Go
Kurt Gassner

First Edition, 2022

Impressum
My-mindguide – The publishing trademarke of trendguide Capital GmbH, Klenzestr. 42a, 80469 Munich, Germany.

Reg. Nr. HRB Munich 206639, VAT 152 123 159, CEO: Kurt Friedrich Gassner
Web: www.my-mindguide.com, mail: gassner@my-mindguide.com

Paperback ISBN: 978-3-98793-016-4
Hardback ISBN: 978-3-98793-017-1

Table of Contents

Let it Go

Let it Go

INTRODUCTION

Humans know how to battle for what is vital to us. They fight to preserve relationships, people, employment, and the status quo. But here's the thing: they don't always put in the same effort to keep us. Holding on to something that is attempting to let go is one of the most painful things we can do. It hurts worse the longer we cling on. The issue is that we have nothing free to seize the things that will be beneficial to us when they come our way.

If you're being knocked down, you'll get through it, but you'll have to let go of whatever it is that's holding you back first. You won't know what awaits you until you open yourself to the world and allow it to show you - which it will.

Consider it like being on a sinking ship. You know you need to let go of something, but you're unable to do it. You're not going to succeed. If you're being honest with yourself, you realize the things weighing you down are dead weights, but can recall a time when having them around felt nice. There hasn't been any happiness like that in a long time — the kind of happiness where you could sit back and relax because you knew there was plenty of it. Meanwhile, your boat continues to sink, and with all of that weight on board, it will never get any closer to land.

I could tell you that the loss and heartache that comes with letting go is part of your 'journey' (though I won't since I despise the word when it's used in that way). I'm confident that the lessons you'll learn will put you on the path to the life you desire. I could tell you all of that, and it would be true, but having been brought to my knees before, I also know that none of that matters when your knuckles are white from holding on.

Letting go of something is a metaphor for removing it from your mental hold rather than your physical grip. Many psychologists define letting go as creating the emotional headspace required to heal from an event or mood. The capacity to let go of personal and intimate familial bonds can be difficult and even catastrophic. That's why we're so emotionally drained while we're grieving. Grief is described as the first step of letting go for various psychiatric reasons. However, grief does not necessitate letting go of something. It might also be the end of a relationship or the loss of a career. On the other hand, people strive to let go of their own emotions, particularly when they have negative impacts, such as feelings of envy or irritation.

One of my greatest personal challenges is letting go.

The concept of "letting go" suggests that you've been clutching on to something. It necessitates the presence of an item; something must be released. We tend to cling to particular expectations, ideas, or ambitions, and this clinging brings us a slew of issues.

What kinds of problems?

Well, here are a few major ways in which our failure to let go can manifest itself:

1. Stress

We frequently become stressed due to our desire for things to be or proceed in a specific way. And when things don't turn out the way we planned, we get even more agitated.

You can probably anticipate that if you are invited to be a bridesmaid at a friend's wedding and your flight is delayed, You ́ll be stressed.

But what happens if the flight is canceled? That is when your anxiety will be at its highest. You'll be scrambling to locate an aircraft or other means of transportation that will get you to your destination in time.

Sadly, things don't continuously turn out how you arranged. And there's a good chance you won't be able to do anything about it.

However, if this is the case, you must:
1) learn to recognize that you can't control or fix the situation.
2) let go of how you want things to be.
3) Accept and embrace the truth of what is because continuing to be stressed and resisting a circumstance beyond your control would just add to your misery.

2. Feeling emotionally drained by events that have occurred, are occurring, or may occur.

We become nervous, upset, angry, or sad much too often as a result of things that (a) have occurred to us, (b) are occurring to us, or (c) may occur to us. We can't seem to get them out of our heads.

For example, you can find yourself enraged about something a previous landlord did to you. Perhaps you become irritated when waiting in line at the post office because someone isn't paying attention and is delaying everyone else. Perhaps you're always concerned about the outcome of a major forthcoming event or commitment.

We tend to choose not to move on, rehashing occasions to us. When we are confronted with inane conditions, we become enraged. And we are always concerned about the future, attempting to think through various situations to better prepare ourselves.

But the truth is that we can't reverse what has already occurred. We can only occasionally influence or modify what is going on in the present. We also cannot foretell or control what will occur in the future.

As a result, we must let go.

We need to let go of everything. Because holding on isn't going to help us.

3. Irritation or frustration with other people
When others don't act in the manner in which we need them to, we become vexed or baffled.

Control is at the heart of this reaction. We want someone to act a specific way, but we can't make them, and our powerlessness and irritation stem from our lack of control.

Furthermore, it typically hurts our connection with the other person when this arises. Our aggravation or frustration with them forms a fissure in our relationship's foundation.

What is the solution? Yes, let go. Allow others to be themselves. Try not to force your views or preferences on them.

This implies you shouldn't maintain a certain level of self-respect or compromise on how you believe you should be treated. I'm not suggesting that you should accept someone without question if they treat you badly or behave badly.

However, it is critical to recognize that we are all human and capable of making errors. You're not flawless, and you shouldn't expect others to be either. Try to tolerate the other person to the degree that their heart is in the right place and they aren't causing significant harm (particularly not purposefully).

Anger seldom helps; instead, it makes the other person feel offended or defensive, making them less inclined to listen to you or alter their mind. Instead, if anything they did hurt or disturbed you, explain why it matters to you. But do so calmly and helpfully.

Whatever the case may be, concentrating on what someone else has done to irritate you will not make you feel better. So let go of your expectations of them and simply let them be themselves.

Holding on to your beliefs about acting will inevitably lead to conflict with reality. You do not influence how other people act. So, rather than allowing it to bring you tension, anger, irritation, or disappointment, let it go. Allow individuals to be who they are and move on.

Not only will you have a better connection with them, but you will also be happier.

4. Struggling with loss or death

When we encounter a loss, whether it is a lost job, a missed opportunity, an illness (i.e., loss of health), or the death of a loved one, we all suffer and grieve. Surprisingly, we also tend to act in ways that prolong our pain out of habit.

For example lets imagine, when your spouse left you, you continuously thought about the loss, his betrayal, and the unbearable grief encompassing you. You couldn't understand why this happened and wished things had turned out differently.

You had an inexplicable urge to learn what was going on in his life after he'd left you for reasons you can't explain, even though each new piece of knowledge seemed to wound you worse than the last. Finding out about his new girlfriend (... yes, honestly) and receiving numerous nasty details of his newest mishaps did not help you feel any better.

Perhaps you sobbed. you were wallowing in your misery. You also indulged in an excessive degree of self-pity.

Finally, you will came to a few realizations. First, you admitted that, despite your marriage, you did not and could never "possess" or "own" your husband. No matter how hard we try, we will never be able to control our beloveds (or anybody else in life, for that matter).

Second, you realized that you needed to shift your viewpoint. You needed to stop seeing your imminent divorce as a rejection or a failure and start seeing it as a freeing event - as a chance to remake myself.

Third, you began to see and comprehend that you needed to let go to be free of your pain. It was time for you to stop looking back and start looking forward. You needed to stop worrying about your husband's new life and focus on yours.

On some level, this is true for all of us anytime we suffer a loss of any type. Everything is brief, after all. To get better at dealing with loss, we must refrain from opposing reality and learn to accept the impermanence of things.

5. Fear

More than likely, you are limited in your approach to life by various anxieties. And each of those worries stems from a desire to keep things the way we want them to be.

Fear toward fizzling, apprehension about relinquishing control, feeling of dread toward forsaking or confiding in others, anxiety toward not being adequate, or feeling of dread toward not being acknowledged for who all of you have a similar arrangement: giving up. By clinging to how you want things to be, you're also clinging to the dread that things won't turn out the way you want them to.

You must let go of your expectations or aspirations. Accept and believe in oneself and the present time (reality).

Then quit attempting to exert control over others and life in general. We may have the delusion that we have control, when, really, we don't. Allow yourself to let go and understand that you have no influence over people or the majority of the environment around you.

Everything is fleeting. Everything. And that's rather frightening. So, when we're presented with change, impermanence, and loss, we resist and try to obtain or impose control over the situation.

Rather than fighting, we must embrace that change is a part of life. We can't change it and resisting it is pointless. We shall only suffer as a result of doing so.

It appears that letting go is a straightforward process. It is, however, anything but. These issues and behaviors that I've discussed have the potential to be firmly established in our minds. And we prefer to defend them and return to them frequently because we believe we are protecting ourselves by doing so.

To let go, you must dig deep and recognize that you do not require protection. You must understand and trust that you will be OK - that everything will be fine.

Let it Go

You know
why it's hard
to be happy?
It's because
we refuse to
let go of
the things that
make us sad.

My-mindguide.com

WHY LETTING GO IS IMPORTANT

"When you decide to take charge of what you do have control over rather than wishing for control over what you don't, incredible changes occur in your life." - Maraboli, Steve.

Consider whatever you're hanging on to and resolve to let go of it. Make a note of it. Is it a dream? Is it resentment? Is it possible that it's hope? Is it a matter of desire? Is it a wish that was never fulfilled? How long have you kept it in your possession? How long has it been bothering you? You must relinquish control.

We've all done it: we cling to something because it means something to us. We can wait years for something, and we are always frustrated when it doesn't happen. Sometimes it's a relationship that we just can't seem to let go of. We believe the spouse was ideal, and there was no way we could find anybody better; hence, we live in regret. It is sometimes a tragedy that causes us to suffer. What about the resentments we harbor? We demand justice now that we've been mistreated, and if it doesn't arrive, we'll live with hatred and bitterness.

At some time in our lives, we have all been confronted with the dilemma of choosing whether to let go or hang on to something or someone. Letting go is one of the hardest things we have to do in our lives, yet it is sometimes the only way to get ourselves to go on. It's extremely tough to let go of things we desperately want to keep. Whether it's items, people, or ideas, we frequently have difficulty admitting that we don't need them since we enjoy them so much. For some reason, we've trained ourselves to believe that we must keep them because the prospect of their leaving or us missing them is simply too painful to bear. But, to see beyond the tough and time-consuming process of letting go, we must take a step back. Instead, we should look ahead to discover what new opportunities will arise due to letting go.

Because we are insecure, some of us may find it difficult to let go. We may believe that nothing will ever be good enough or better than what we currently have. We must recognize that this is just not the case. As long as we maintain our optimism, greater things will begin to come our way. We must not let our connection to something obstruct our letting go procedures. We will take time to ponder if we genuinely love ourselves. Is what we have adequate for our needs? If there is even a speck of uncertainty, we should start thinking about letting go of whatever it is. We are in control of our fates. How much we develop and prosper is ultimately determined by our decisions. If we continue to be stationary in our lives, we will now grow. We must practice analyzing what we have and choosing if it is truly worth holding on to allow ourselves to grow. I can tell you from personal experience that it will be difficult to be honest with yourself and decide that something needs to go. Still, if you allow yourself time to adjust to the notion, you will never look back because you will realize how taking this step helps your progress and life.

Asking yourself, “If I let this go, what will it create a place for?” is one technique to start letting go. The overall response will almost certainly be something of equal or better worth. The most simple example will be if you’ve been holding on to a sweater that you’ve had for years but never worn. It’s is one of your favorites. It was a birthday present from your best buddy. If you let it go, you’ll free up a hanger in your wardrobe, which you may use to hang a new piece of clothes you might find the next time you’re out shopping. This piece of apparel will most likely fit you better and will be more fashionable. It is a better option for you. I realize this is a very simple example, but the concept remains the same in more difficult cases. When we give up something, we never fully lose our love for it; it only evolves into a love for something else. This is feasible because we’ve cleared the way for something new to arrive. It’s critical to remember that even after we’ve let go of something we care about, we always get to have the memories we have of it.

Allowing yourself to let go does not have to imply forgetting. It entails surrendering something’s capacity to negatively impact you so that you are not swamped with unpleasant emotions when you recall it. Is it possible for you to overlook something? Sure, but you’re also aware that you now have more place in your life for better, more pleasant things. If you decide to let go of a loved one because liking and having them in your life is no longer beneficial, letting go does not mean forgetting all that has ever occurred to that person. It entails separating yourself from that individual and fondly recollecting moments involving that person while remaining unaffected by the fact that you no longer have them in your life. This is, without a doubt, a process, and it may not always be simple. However, letting go of that person allows you to redirect your existing love toward other individuals who could be a better fit for you right now in your life. If you're having trouble getting through this because you're missing that person in a way that makes you feel sad or lonely, refocus your thoughts on the boundless possibilities that your life now has room for.

We have the power to choose what we let go of and what we hang on to, and our choices will ultimately determine the paths that our lives take. If you stay at a job you don't enjoy for too long, it may damage your happiness and overall well-being; but, if you let go of it, even if it's scary and slightly sad, you'll be opening up your life to new options and experiences that were previously unavailable. It's tough to let go of anything you actually love or care about or even something that simply provides you with comfort. Keep in mind that everyone has this problem at some time in their lives. If you're having trouble letting go of something that no longer serves you well, be gentle to yourself and forgive yourself.

To begin, stay in the present and ask yourself, "Is loving this person, object, or concept helping me and making me happy right now?" If you answered yes, you may not be able to or need to let go just yet. If the answer is no, ask yourself, "Could letting go of this item, person, or concept lead to my having a brighter and happier life in the future?" If you answered yes, or even if you answered maybe, you should think about starting the process of letting go. Do it, even if it feels terrifying, and even though you know you'll miss whatever you're letting go of. Better things will come your way. We don't lose or destroy love; it simply takes on a new form.

When I was in high school, I stumbled across the following quotation and thought it was interesting. I'm not sure

I comprehended it at the time, but pondering on it has greatly aided me as time has passed. I hope that reading it will also assist and encourage you.

"All the skill of living resides in a perfect blending of letting go and clinging on."

-Havelock Ellis

Why is letting go difficult?

We understand the significance of letting go of the things that hold us back, so why is it so difficult? It all boils down to accepting responsibility. It appears that blaming conditions on individuals, events, and things is more convenient than admitting we are mistaken.

While we should acknowledge and affirm the past's influence on you, blaming it for your current sentiments takes away your authority. You relinquish authority to something that will never assist you by doing so. The past is gone, and regardless of the amount you wish for it, it won't ever have the option to recuperate you.

Letting go of the trauma

Accept that the trials of the period were beyond your control to let go. You couldn't have done anything more to change the circumstance. The past has passed, and you should not punish yourself by dwelling on it. Trauma stole everything away from us, and you should regain everything throughout your rehabilitation. As a result, letting go entails arming yourself with current tools and opting to live your best life today.

Reasons to Let Go of the Past

It appears that letting go is a difficult process for many people. The reason for this remains a mystery. In our lives, we all go through a variety of events. Each stage of our lives presents new difficulties and chances to master certain activities, develop new abilities, explore new sides of ourselves, and learn more about who we are connected to people and the world around us. Often, we take pleasure in our accomplishments and how we attain our objectives. It feels nice to let go and go on in such a situation. When we're content with the way our lives are turning out, it's much easier to let go and be open to whatever happens next.

In our lives, we will confront times of extreme difficulty or stress, times when we will feel fear and anxiety. We don't always know where we're headed or how we're going to get there. Sometimes, no matter how hard we try, we just can't seem to get out of a rut. That happens all the time, whether you want it to or not. In fact, it happens to the vast majority of us on a regular basis. It's quite OK to feel lost and confused about the future. Hopefully, our challenges and problems will be resolved at some point, and we will be able to go on.

But what happens if you become stuck and can't get out? You just can't stop pondering and worrying over the past—what was, what couldn't happen, the chance that slipped away, the person you love who doesn't love you the same way, the challenging relationship that continues to test your integrity and health. You just can't let go of all the things you thought would make you happy, all the things you expected, all the hopes and dreams you yearned for but didn't come true! You're locked in the feelings of that moment, constantly rehearsing the anguish, remorse, humiliation, sense of loss, and so on.

I know it's difficult to let go of everything you've invested in and are adamantly committed to, but you must let go because, as painful as it may be, it's the only way to progress.

So, here are a few ideas to get you started on moving ahead and maybe letting go of what no longer serves you.

The past is done.

No matter how long you spend thinking about it or how much effort you put into it, it doesn't matter. You have no control over what happened, but you do have control over your reaction to it. You may reframe your thoughts and feelings more positively to reflect lessons learned and wisdom acquired rather than thinking negatively about the past—your disappointment, grief, and struggle to have something that was not intended to be yours. You can accept that you are a work in progress and that what has occurred to you represents your current growth stage. You learn to regard these past occurrences as stepping stones toward your future as you mature as a person.

Self-limiting beliefs prevent you from letting go.

You restrict your capacity to develop and evolve when you assume that what you're experiencing is the only option you have and the only time you'll have it. You miss out on many chances when you limit your conviction in your ability. When you think narrowly, you miss opportunities to try new things and achieve. You take away your power to be the "master" of your creativity. You are robbing yourself of the chance to aid in the realization of your deepest aspirations.

You make room for something new to happen when you let go.

It's the equivalent of having a junk drawer full of things you don't use or require. Do you know what's on the inside? Take a step back and evaluate your emotional, psychological, physical, and spiritual requirements. Do the things that used to make sense in your life still make sense to you? Are you clinging to the past out of nostalgia? Are you worried you'll forget if you let go? You create a large room for anything to happen when you clean away the wreckage of the past.

Your past is not your identity.

Yes, it's a part of your past and who you are, but it's not who you are. Your life experiences are a reflection of who you are. Things happen, but how they happen and how they show themselves is uniquely colored by each individual. You leave your mark. Your identity is just as important to your future as it is to your history. When you stay stuck in the past, you won't live in the present and into the future.

Letting go is the cornerstone of change.

All preceding statements refer to this, but it's critical to state it explicitly. Some individuals just go through life's motions. They appear to be active participants in life, yet they are not. They're thinking, feeling, hoping, and dreaming about a life that should have happened but didn't. It was a complete waste of time. You'll never know your strength, courage, or ability to live life to the fullest. You are surrendering to fear of the unknown and possibly failure when you refuse to let go. When you refuse to let go, you restrict yourself from living a full and abundant life.

You will be stronger.

It's not simple to let go of previous battles, old habits, and individuals who aren't looking out for your best interests. It necessitates that we step outside of our comfort zones. This is why many of us want to keep things as they are. We keep making excuses for why we can't let go of their history. Choosing to let go, on the other hand, will make you stronger and more secure. It engages you to zero in on what you truly need to accomplish to inhabit the time and become who you really are. You'll discover how to overcome each new difficulty that comes your way. You will be able to take control of your objectives and your life due to this.

You'll feel liberated in a way you never have before.

Imagine carrying a hefty backpack full of rocks through life. They each represent every awful experience you've had, dragging you down. Making you feel trapped and preventing you from experiencing your life to the fullest.

By deciding to toss each rock away and release it, you will get a new sense of freedom that will permeate every element of your life.

You can appreciate yourself.

Your past has formed you into who you are today. Recognizing this is an excellent first step in appreciating and accepting your narrative. Nobody is flawless, and we all have a history of dealing with it.

You make room in your heart for the great things the world has to offer today when you forgive yourself and let go of all that occurred yesterday.

You may channel your energy towards achieving the objectives and desires that bring you joy.

Let it Go

JUST
LET IT
GO

SIGNS THAT TELL YOU IT'S TIME TO LET GO

One of the most difficult aspects of life is letting go. Because your emotions tend to confuse your thinking and make it difficult for you to concentrate, it appears that the skill of letting go might be perplexing and tough.

"You will discover that letting go of things is vital simply because they are weighty." So, let them go, let them go." C. JoyBell

Should you let go of someone, particularly your current job, old sentiments, or resentment? Should you hang on and let them completely swallow you? These indicators are telling you to let go and live:

1. You're supposed to put your ideas aside and transform into someone you're not.
Personal values and vision are the things that define who you are in this life. Let go if your career, partner, or acquaintance compels you to be someone you're not. You'll never be completely yourself regardless.

2. Your confidence is constantly betrayed.

When you fall in love with an idea, a person, an event, or a feat, you become vulnerable. They say that loving someone entails allowing them to harm you, but you're trusting them not to do so, right? So, if your boyfriend constantly hurts you or your loved ones consistently ignore your sentiments, it's time to let them go. What makes you believe the pain will go away if you keep hanging on?

3. Staying in it makes you feel broken, unhappy, and frustrated all of the time.

You despise your work, your relationship, or your company. You have no idea why you entered this contest in the first place. You despise the people you're with and the things you're doing. You're not motivated to keep going.

4. You feel inferior.

Your self-worth is constantly undervalued. You never seem to be in a good mood. It's as though you're taken for granted all of the time. Everyone expects you to show up there, but when you do, you're treated as if you're already there! If it appears like you are the only one chasing, please do yourself a favor and quit. This is like constantly berating yourself—just let go.

5. You defend why it's worthwhile to hang on when it's not.

"Oh, he forgot about my birthday since she was so preoccupied..."

"He never introduced me to his buddies since he claims they are no longer his true pals..."

"I'm sure my business partner didn't want to bankrupt us; I'm sure he has a plan..."

"I love my job, even though I'm always pressured and never have time to spend with my family...right?"

Examine yourself and pay attention to what you're saying: do you honestly believe what you're saying? No. So relax.

6. You can't recall the last time you felt joyful.

When was the last time you were happy—as in, completely pleased, fulfilled, and at ease in your skin? Don't put too much pressure on yourself, my friend. If you're unable to recall anything, it's time to let go and go on.

7. You notice that you're the one who constantly has to make concessions.

Are you the one that constantly has to sacrifice extra time? More cash? Is there anything else I can do? Do you always seem to be the one who is in greater pain? More annoyance? Do you want to feel even more anxious? Stop pursuing yourself and do yourself a favor.

8. It's been a while since you utilized your words to express yourself.

Why are you still hanging on if your ideas are continually silenced and your feelings are ignored? You know you're capable of more.

9. Because it hurts too much, you refuse to accept the present.

You opt to live in the past rather than face the present predicament since wonderful memories console you there. You live in denial and attempt to convince yourself that everything will work out in the end, even though every fiber of your being knows it won't.

10. Inconsistency exists—every time.

It's all too easy to take the back seat and allow yourself to be influenced when the person you're dealing with has a knack for words. Do not forget that words alone will not cure every problem. It's typically a negative omen if he says one thing and then does another.

Your business partner promises to solve things but never follows through? Allow yourself to relax.

Your sweetheart swears he'll never cheat on you again, but he does. Allow yourself to relax.

Your loved ones claim that they will act in your best interests, but they don't? Allow yourself to relax.

11 You've already used all of your efforts, yet nothing has changed.

When you've done everything you can when all the promises you've been given have been broken when it's no longer worth your time, money, tears, or aggravation...

Allow yourself to relax.

You aren't living in a fantasy world. Promises are frequently broken. Lovers harm you. Your business partners can deceive you. Not every person is looking out for you.

Remove the harmful belief that staying on would make things better.

Allow yourself to let go and live. You know you've earned it.

Signs It Is Time to Let Go of Your Relationship

It's all about striking a balance between clinging on and letting go in life. We continuously attempt to make the right choice, but making the perfect decision isn't always simple, especially concerning individuals we love.

We invest a lot of our emotions, time, and energy in relationships, and the more we invest, the more difficult it is to let go. We don't let go for various reasons; we don't let go because we're afraid of the unknown; we don't let go because we're afraid of being alone; the reasons are numerous, but the ultimate effect is the same: we're unhappy.

While lying, cheating, and disrespect are among the most prevalent and serious causes of breakups, we rarely recognize that these are symptoms of various underlying problems. We often turn a blind eye to many things that seem frightening in the hopes that things would improve, but as the relationship deteriorates, the harm gets more serious. No amount of salvaging will be able to restore it.

Knowing when to let go will save you a lot of heartaches and allow you to move ahead with a more positive mindset. There is a possibility that you need to let go if you feel any of these symptoms.

1. You are not yourself.

You are not right if you continuously have to pretend to be someone you are not out of fear of being criticized or misunderstood.

2. You are not genuinely happy.

Here, we're talking about happiness, not simply getting along or surviving. A relationship shouldn't be boring or lifeless when things are going well.

3. You want different things.

It will be difficult for couples to meet halfway if they are not on the same page and their aims and ambitions vastly differ. They'll both be caught in a relationship where, instead of living life together, they'll each choose their own way, eventually drifting apart.

4. You're constantly chastised and rarely acknowledged.

If your spouse frequently criticizes you in public or in private, whether it's for your appearance, conduct, or views and beliefs, it suggests they can't see the good in you.

5. The zeal and the good times are no longer there.

Boredom and dullness take over the relationship when the passion has faded. This is one of the reasons why many individuals cheat and look for someone else to fill the emotional void.

6. You are lonely most of the time.

A solid relationship is one in which the accomplices are content to impart their lives to another through various difficulties. If you feel like you're going through everything alone in a relationship, it's a dead giveaway that it's already shattered.

7. You're putting in too much effort and making a lot of concessions.

Relationships should be established on an equitable exchange of goods and services. If you're making all of the effort to keep the relationship going on your own, you're certain to become resentful and dissatisfied.

8. You're always coming up with reasons and justifications for your actions.

If you feel compelled to continuously come up with excuses for why you're being ignored and defend them in front of your parents and friends, you're merely blinding yourself to the truth.

9. You're always in a conflict.

If you can't communicate with each other and wind up fighting and arguing, it's a sign that you're not compatible and don't understand one other well enough. It might also be an indication of bottled-up rage and irritation.

10. The connection depletes your energy.

It should never seem like work or an obligation to be near the person you love; it should offer you warmth, joy and elevate your spirits. If you're in a relationship that makes you feel sick all the time and makes you need some alone time, you're in the wrong location with the wrong person.

11. You're weighed down and suffocating.

You're under a lot of stress because of their presence. You don't feel at ease among them and feel compelled to explain yourself all of the time. You set forth some part of the energy to make your time together pleasant, yet you never anticipate seeing them again.

12. In the connection, you are afraid.

Because their reactions usually frighten and make you uneasy, you think twice before speaking or reacting a certain way. You need to break free from the bonds of this connection if you walk on eggshells around your lover and are constantly scared that what you say or do will upset them.

13. You've been treated with contempt and cruelty.
Abuse and disrespect have no place in healthy relationships; it is not feasible. Cut it off immediately.

14. You're in it in the hopes that things will improve.
You've been trying to mend things for a long time, yet you still know and feel in your heart that something is wrong. In such a circumstance, you are just holding out a sliver of hope that they will change, either because you are waiting for things to improve or because you believe this is the best you can get.

15. You're being held back by your relationship.
The appropriate partner will encourage and drive you to achieve your objectives and goals, and they will never stand in the way of your professional or personal growth and evolution.

16. Their baggage is causing problems in their relationship.
Are you head over heels in love with someone who is severely damaged? Someone who carries baggage from previous relationships, battles with familial difficulties, struggles with rage or insecurity, struggles with substance misuse, and so on? Someone who is difficult to be around due to their injuries?

Many of us stick with individuals even if they aren't making us happy. We feel that unless we support them, they will not improve.

And while those are excellent ideas, I realize they are motivated by love, and I believe you should consider releasing them for their benefit.

Many of us who stay because we believe we can help or they need us perpetuate the harmful conduct. We tend to overcompensate for their harm by excusing their drinking or transforming ourselves into someone other than ourselves to avoid triggering them about past relationships. Who is the one who walks on tiptoe to avoid an angry outburst?

Trying to help your loved one in this way may be understandable, but it's not helping your loved one in any way. They could be making things worse.

You can genuinely offer your damaged person a chance to get well if you can find the fortitude to let them go if you can tell them that you love them and want to assist and support them, but all you see is them growing worse your relationship getting more toxic.

People are far more inclined to seek assistance if you let them go, and they discover that they are not only alone but also that they are not in a relationship where someone is overcompensating for their problems.

I know you're concerned that if you let them go, they'll mend themselves and find someone else with whom to live happily ever after. And that's a possibility. My advice is to let go of the dream that they will be fixed and you will be able to live a happy life. You're going to be miserable.

If your partner is struggling in a way that is causing your relationship to suffer, consider letting them leave for their benefit to have a healthy and happy life. And you do as well.

17. You don't love them as much as you should be.

My client Monica told me: "When I was married and miserable, I fantasized about abandoning my spouse so that he could find someone who made him happy. Even though we were having difficulties, I still loved him, and the thought of him being with someone else made me sick to my stomach.

So I hung on for selfish reasons, and we both ended up miserable."

Allow someone you love to depart if you know you don't love them enough. Allow them to be happy, discover genuine love, and not live a life that isn't as fulfilling as they deserve.

I understand how frightening it is, and I understand how concerned you are that you will never find love again if you let go of this person. And I understand. That said, I can almost guarantee that if you don't let go of this individual, you'll be doomed to years of misery.

I can also guarantee that you will find someone else to adore if you let them go.

So, if you look at the person you're with and don't feel enough love for them, let them go. Allow you and your partner to be happy.

After we separated, I knew that both my ex and I were fortunate enough to discover our true mates and are now enjoying happy lives. That gut sensation is still with me, but I'm pleased things turned out the way they did.

18. You are yo-yoing.
It's normal to have second thoughts about a romantic partner, especially if your feelings for them are mutual and you've been dating for some time.

Perhaps you're dissatisfied with how they treat you, or you're restless, or you'd like to spend more time with your pals.

As a result, you may inform your contact that you require some time. You either leave the house, stop calling, or disappear. Your actions have brought an end to our partnership.

Then you go back to them a day, a week, or a month later. Perhaps you're hoping things will turn out differently, or perhaps you're lonely, or perhaps hanging out with your buddies has become tedious.

After a while, you realize that nothing has changed and that you still don't love them. And then you're gone.

This is known as yo-yoing, and it may be quite damaging to the individual who is left behind. I have numerous customers that are forced to yo-yoing, and I can assure you that it kills their self-esteem in every case. They're left with the sensation that they're not good enough, and they're left wondering why you can't love them as much as they love you. They strive to modify who they are in the hopes of making things better this time. They are bothered by what their ex-partner does after they break up.

If you find yourself coming and departing with your partner, it's time to put an end to it! Try to see beyond your own self-centered desires and let them go. Allow them to rediscover themselves, realize they are sufficient, and stop worrying about what you will do next.

If you can accomplish this, you and your partner will have an opportunity to be happy and discover love instead of being caught on the gerbil wheel of attempting to fix something that isn't broken.

Relationships should bring out the best in us, assist us in growing and evolving, and most importantly, assist us in uncovering our genuine selves. Your companion should make you feel at ease, like a home away from home. If you're in a relationship with someone who doesn't give you something to look forward to every day, you're with the wrong person.

Let it Go

Whatever's bothering you . . .

Let it go!

Doreen Virtue

BENEFITS OF LETTING GO

Much has been written about letting go of a burden to lighten our weight or letting go of an outdated, outmoded behavior or habit to embrace a new and better one. We may have grown connected to what we feel is great and works for us, so letting go is not as simple as it seems. Letting go of long-held views and ideas may feel like we're losing something valuable when, in reality, we're making way for a new concept that's even better. Take into account the following:

- Letting go of negative ideas and feelings is like letting go of a harmful poison; our brains, bodies, and spirits become healthier and more productive.

- Letting go of a failed and damaged relationship opens the door to previously unimagined opportunities.

- Letting rid of worn-out clothing or a pair of shoes allows you to replace it with something more fitting and attractive.

- Letting rid of a set, rigid routine while being predictable, safe, and comfortable allows for more freedom, flexibility, and creativity.

- Freeing up time and space by letting go of certain tangible belongings that require upkeep and administration frees up time and space for other, possibly postponed, pursuits.

- Letting goes and saying goodbye to a loved one is a celebration of life and a way to respect the memories of someone significant in your life.

- Letting goes of the past allows us to focus on the now and plan for the future.

1. YOU REDISCOVER YOUR WORTH
When you let go of a painful circumstance, you may take a step back and realize that you deserved so much more to begin with. Leaving a job that makes you unhappy might help you understand that other career options are a better match for you. Allowing yourself to let go of someone who takes you for granted allows you to invest in individuals who value you and provide value to your relationships.

2. OTHER THINGS ARE APPRECIATED IN YOUR LIFE.
Allowing yourself to let go of what you can't control will help you see the brighter side of life. When things don't go as planned, there's always something to be thankful for. Allowing yourself to move on from a toxic relationship reveals the people and qualities important to you.

3. INVESTIGATE YOURSELF TO DEVELOP YOURSELF.
You'll be able to see your true self more clearly once you let go of the things preventing you from seeing it. We can destroy our pleasure by clinging to people who aren't healthy for us. We are

prevented from exploring other connections in our own lives that may provide fresh possibilities for us to grow and develop if we do not let go. Change necessitates taking an honest look at ourselves and moving on, which is a lot simpler when you don't feel compelled to micromanage every detail of your life.

4. YOU FIND ACCEPTANCE AND PEACE

Accepting that something is beyond our control may be uplifting and serene. When you fully accept and let go of a situation, you stop fighting, rejecting, worrying, manipulating, and overthinking. Instead, focus your energy on moving forward constructively and healthily. As a consequence, you're at ease, peaceful, and ready to take on whatever life throws at you.

5. YOU ARE NO LONGER CONTROLLED

You'll notice that after you've walked away from a poisonous scenario, it no longer occupies your time and attention. You're less preoccupied with it, fresh and interesting experiences divert your thoughts, and you have a sense of relief from its hold on you. When you genuinely let go, you will discover that your life is fantastic, healthy, and stress-free in ways you could never have imagined before.

Benefits of Letting Go of Items

The moonlight shone through the windows when I awoke, spreading silver shadows over the room. As I glanced over to the watch, which read 3:30 a.m., the air mattress seemed a little mushy. We were attempting to sell our home. All of the furniture and other goods that might be given had already been done. The remainder of the artifacts were regrettably discarded in a landfill. The 1500+ square foot mansion needed four huge trucks to empty. Before the sale, I stayed there for a week on an air mattress, with a hot water kettle, ketchup, and ice in the fridge. Of course, there was a functional TV and Wi-Fi, essential' needs.' That's when it dawned on me: less is more. We can do without a lot of things. We amass stuff,' give in to using buying as an emotional release, hoard items in closets, pack cupboards, and buy more furniture to house it all, leading to an endless cycle. In many ways, letting go may prove to be cathartic.

You have a lighter feeling. We carry our belongings on our shoulders and backs. No, I'm not talking about physically; I'm talking about emotionally. The overflowing closets, the monthly storage costs at the 'climate controlled' facility, the outfits with price tags still attached, the unopened wine glasses, and the drawer that won't open are all on the brain's radar. We transport these items as cargoes daily. The weight lightens as you let go. You have the energy to go further since the weight is removed off your shoulders.

You can assist others. Giving brings some of the greatest delights in life. Giving is preferable to receiving. Things you don't need, and even things you believe you need (but don't), can benefit others. Give your belongings to a charity of your choice. Make someone else happy.

You can make the most of what you have. Be honest, you'll never play the fifty board games you've gathered in the basement closet. Finding, picking, dusting, and then discovering that a vital item to play the game is missing is a tedious procedure. The good times will roll if you merely have two board games that are well-kept and conveniently available. You'll know where to find that beloved book, that particular coffee cup, or that present from Grandma if you have less but are organized.

You can earn money. Someone else's trash might be a valuable asset. Hire a local selling agency, organize a garage sale, or sell online through various websites. You get to declutter your house and turn trash into money.

You start to get organized. Clearing away the stuff you don't need allows you to make more room. Things can be placed where they need to be in the space. The kitchen will no longer resemble the Bermuda Triangle, with everything jumbled up across cabinets. You'll know just where to look for the ice cream scoop and that strange tool for making potato cringles.

You're a cleaner person. When you first declutter your closet, you'll be sitting on a mound of clothing or boxes, but as you declutter, you'll be cleaning, renewing, and sterilizing it. The air in an uncluttered house will be cleaner, smell nicer, and feel healthier.

You make a decision and then evaluate it. Do you need to retain all fifty of Grandma's belongings? Is this item I'm looking at significant? Is it necessary in the physical sense? Is it possible for me to live without it? You will examine your decisions without becoming too philosophical. What is most essential to me, and what do I require in the future? What does the future hold for me? On this subject, there will be more to come. Just declutter for the time being.

LETTING GO OF CONTROL CAN HELP YOU ENJOY LIFE

It's normal to feel the urge to be in command. It's something we all desire, and it makes us feel the greatest when we know exactly what's going on in all of our lives. It's crucial to remember, though, that we'll never be able to manage everything. When things don't go the way we want them to, we experience unpleasant feelings.

There are numerous methods to boost your pleasure in life, but letting go of control is one of the simplest and most tangible. Why should we do it, and where do we start? We'll go over all you need to know about why you should quit attempting to control every aspect of your life and how to get there.

Why Do We Feel the Need to Control?

The need to control our environment and events is deeply embedded in our psyche. The more we understand our surroundings, the more secure we feel. Conversely, the less we know, the more terrified we get. Dread is at the basis of the need to control—specifically, the fear of what may happen if we lose control.

How Attempts to Control Negatively Affect Our Lives

It's natural to want to be in charge of everything, but that doesn't mean it's a good idea. Trying to manage everything might backfire in various ways. Let's look at a few of the most popular.

Increased Stress And Anxiety

Those who strive to manage everything are more likely to be stressed and anxious. A person's blood pressure might increase just by feeling out of control when it feels important to be in it.

According to research, when things don't go as planned, persons who feel the need to control suffer more than those who don't feel the need to control.

There is a decrease in satisfaction.

Feeling a need for control and not having it might lead to dissatisfaction.

According to one study, "subjects who scored high on a measure of a general desire for control reported higher levels of discomfort and perceived the room as more crowded than subjects who scored low on the desire for control at both levels of density reported higher levels of discomfort and perceived the room as more crowded."

The act of feeling a desire for control resulted in a less pleasant setting for those who prioritized it over those who didn't.

More Criticism

Because there is no way to control everything, being too concerned with things outside your control might lead to increasing criticism of everything that occurs. After all, if you don't control the outcomes you want, it's natural to dislike them.

On the other hand, being more critical might make us more neurotic, producing a never-ending and spiraling loop in which we become increasingly dissatisfied with our lives. Criticizing others may be harmful to persons who are depressed or anxious, prompting them to condemn themselves even more.

What Can You Gain By Giving Up Control?

Given how detrimental the urge for control can be to our lives, it should come as no surprise that giving it up has a lot of benefits.

Michael Singer's book "The Surrender Experiment" is one example of this, in which the author discusses how his life improved once he quit attempting to control everything. Here are some of the advantages of letting go of the urge to be in charge of everything.

Increased Peace And Relaxation

Proponents of submitting and using a technique like Singer's talk of enhanced serenity and calm due to doing so. This makes sense when you realize that attempting to control everything leads to worry and anxiety and that serenity and relaxation are opposed.

Preparedness for the Unexpected is Improved.

You'll be in a better position to deal with whatever the situation's conclusion is if you're less fixated on a specific outcome. People who have abandoned their control may simply handle anything life throws at them.

They are better able to go with the flow since they have less attachment. This implies you'll be fine no matter what happens in life, rather than basing your sense of well-being on certain results that may be beyond your control.

Enhanced Connections With Self and Others

In the same way that is attempting to control everything makes you harsher on yourself and others, relinquishing control allows you to connect with others deeper. That's because you're not basing your self-love and acceptance of others on certain results.

You can love more freely if you just let people be who they are circumstance. This is true for both loving others and loving oneself.

How to Let Go Of Control

Assume you've determined that being at ease and connected to people is preferable to being anxious and critical. If that's the case, you're certainly curious about how to go about letting go of your desire for control. The suggestions below will assist you in getting started on this pleasant route.

Anything you can do to help you feel more at ease with your lack of control is fantastic. It might be big or tiny, done frequently or just when necessary. To assist you in navigating your new trip, we recommend using one of the resources listed below.

Discern What You Can and Can't Control

There's no way to relinquish control unless you realize where it's required in your life. Take stock of your current situation. Consider which aspects of your life you control and which you don't.

Once you've figured out which circumstances fit into each category, commit to handling the ones over which you don't or won't have control differently than you have in the past. This includes detaching yourself from results and treating others differently when they don't act the way you want.

To feel less anxious about the many possible outcomes, it may be good to think through the scenarios you have no influence over. Do your best to feel at ease with each one as you consider it, knowing that it is beyond your control, that you are protected, and that you will be OK regardless of how things turn out.

Practice Mindfulness

It's all about being present in mindfulness. Being present and embracing everything wonderful as it happens will assist you in achieving the experience of surrender. It allows you to control your emotions, which is particularly beneficial if you suffer from a need for control. It also lowers stress, which rises as the urge for control grows.

Journal

Writing out your emotions might help you relax and de-stress. You may be able to think about things more deeply when you journal than if you merely think about them. Journaling can assist those who feel the need to be in control to go through various outcomes and provide an outlet for their sentiments without allowing them to intensify and expand.

Get Support From Loved Ones

Finally, you do not have to go through this alone! There's a good chance you have at least one loved one who attempts to micromanage every aspect of life. You can contact them and inform them that you are on a mission to submit and relinquish power. Invite them to join you, and then meet or chat with them regularly to discuss how your progress.

Lean on someone in your life who has previously relinquished control and experienced the calm that comes with it for assistance. Inquire for advice, offer your own experiences, and take notes on what they've done.

The need for control is normal, yet it may also complicate our lives. With these suggestions, you may start living a happy life.

HOW TO LET GO OF ALL CLUTTERS IN YOUR LIFE.

Do you have dishes in the sink, mounds of dirty clothes heaped high, blankets and pillows strewn around the floor, closets in disorder, too much stuff in the garage, and an unfathomable amount of unneeded goods strewn about the house?

We live in a materialistic world that teaches us that the more stuff we have, the happier we must be, whereas, in reality, clutter may lead to stagnated energy and excessive tension.

Uncontrolled purchasing impulses, emotional attachment to things, sentimental mementos, dread of getting rid of things, and the urge to cling on to previous memories are just a few of the reasons why we prefer to infuse our possessions with our emotions.

Because throwing things away may be difficult and might mean losing the past and giving up on our future, we frequently hold on to things in the hopes that they will come in handy someday, but in reality, they add to our mental and emotional stress.

What is clutter?
Clutter, according to Dictionary.com, is disorderly or overflowing with items. It can also refer to a state or condition of being perplexed.

On the other hand, Clutter can relate to emotional and mental "baggage," as well as untidiness and an excessive number of physical things.

Although we usually associate clutter with tangible items, mental and emotional clutter may take up just as much room as physical clutter.

Clutter comprises old habits, resentment, foggy thoughts, tumultuous relationships, outstanding financial obligations, a broken vase, out-of-style clothing, and any other "thing" you have to handle.

Even the cleanest of homes can become congested due to clutter.

According to Kerry Thomas, a speaker, and professional organizer, in a recent TED Ideas article. Her physical rooms had always been spotless, which is unsurprising considering her career. Still, in this heartbreaking article, she recounts that she felt overwhelmed by clutter even after recovering from major surgery. It wasn't the physical sort, though.

"My life appeared to be going well, and I was getting a lot of praises," Thomas says, "but I was trapped." "Why? There was a lot of emotional baggage in my life. It was full of anxieties and worries, such as, "What if the operation doesn't work?" and "What if my heart breaks again?" There's also the issue of guilt. "'How come I'm still here when others aren't?" I questioned."

We don't feel overwhelmed merely because our closets, inboxes, or to-do lists are full (though that is undoubtedly a contributing factor). Our thoughts and consciences are equally as untidy and stressful as our bodies. The following are the four primary categories of clutter:

Physical clutter.

This "is the standard things we think of — overstuffed closets, garages that can't hold vehicles, storage facilities that have grown into a multibillion-dollar business in the United States alone."

Mental clutter.

This "maybe your worries, your to-do list, what's on the news, or anything else that keeps you up at night."

Emotional clutter.

"Negative habits and beliefs you don't even aware you're carrying around" make up this form of clutter, which might include "can't statements" like "I can't lose weight" or "I can't quit my job and start my own business."

Spiritual clutter.

This is defined as "a lack of forgiveness or peace."

Working through these other, less tangible clutter requires both elbow grease and emotional exertion, just as clearing away physical clutter does.

With the physical clutter, you must box it up, bag it, and get it to a donation center, the curb, or wherever it is you can dispose of it. You'll need to take action for the other types of clutter, which might include talking to a close friend, getting out in nature, meditating, or writing. Put another way, do something, move forward, make a decision, and take action, no matter how small. You will be rewarded with momentum from the cosmos.

Other things that might be considered clutter include:

- Does not have a place to land or live
- It no longer serves a purpose to you
- Is broken or is it in need of repair
- Is messy
- Is disorganized or chaotic
- Is stagnant
- Has become challenging to manage

EMOTIONAL CLUTTER

We all experience emotions that we don't always manage well.

Feelings of resentment or wrath, loss, dread or concern, anxieties, and guilt or remorse are examples of "emotional clutter."

Research on human emotion is not a precise science, according to psychologists. Self-awareness of the interplay between body and mind is widely accepted as a beginning point for managing intruding emotions. It may be simpler to avoid the influence of emotional clutter if we are proficient at identifying different sorts of emotional clutter strewn over our minds.

Our emotions guide our lives.

It's worthwhile to consider how emotions influence our life. Our primary emotions are the emotional responses when confronted with a situation. They're frequently followed by a subsequent feeling that's more protected. We are sometimes just mindful of the secondary feeling. This might be the rage that masks a deeper fear, embarrassment that masks grief, or anxiety that masks a deeper dread.

These emotional reactions directly impact what happens next in our interactions with the world and other people.

Secondary emotions frequently generate emotional clutter, making it difficult to solve problems or make decisions. These deeper layers of sensations are often unseen by us. Nonetheless, they have the potential to have a significant impact on our lives.

What Is Emotional Clutter?

How many of these thoughts have run through your mind?

"I should be more ______."
"I'm so overwhelmed."
"I can't handle everything that's on my plate."
"I'm not appreciated."
"I do everything around here."
"He should know how I feel."
"I'm a bad [mom / partner / sibling / friend]."
"I can't do this." (whatever this is, in your situation)
"My kids deserve someone better."
"I'm gonna lose my mind!"
"I have no self-control."
"I'm not [confident, successful, smart, or thin] enough."
These are what I refer to as "emotional clutter."

The continuous, negative ideas about ourselves, our lives, and others are emotional clutter.

Emotional clutter, like physical clutter, drags us down. But although getting rid of your physical clutter might make you feel lighter and freer.

It will give you that sensation a hundred times over if you clear up your emotional clutter.

Consider what you could achieve if you let go of or rewrite the most typical negative scripts in your thoughts. Consider how that might affect your FEELINGS daily.

The Issue Is...

The issue is... Negative ideas are very appealing to your brain!

It's become so accustomed to thinking them that they may begin to seem like facts about yourself or the people in your life, rather than just ideas.

Let's pretend you're out on a hike.

Consider the route you'd take down a mountain. That road will become increasingly evident as you continue.

You'll compact the earth and trample some of the underbrush, making it much simpler to follow that trail the next time you trek there.

This is how our brains work.

The more you think about something, the clearer the route in your brain gets.

Good news: We can change the negative pathways by becoming conscious and repeating ourselves. With our newfound freedom, we'll be able to sculpt a new path down the mountainside.

Life's difficulties can produce a lot of turbulence and make it tough to stay up and track. When we're confronted with hardship, we're also confronted with a slew of options, feelings, and ideas that might obscure our judgment or make it difficult to absorb. We must learn to declutter our emotional space and go back to the base of who we are and what we want to live happier, healthier, and more satisfying lives.

Allowing emotional baggage to distract or derail you is not healthy. You may recover your real core by letting go of the people, situations, and feelings that no longer provide you joy, satisfaction, or support. And return your attention to the issues that truly matter today and in the future. Find the bravery and strength to become a more active participant in your life. Declutter your mind and emotions so you may live a life that is free and true to your most profound convictions.

It's easy to get lost in the clutter.

It's all too easy to become lost in life's chaos, and when we do, it may utterly overwhelm who we are and what we want in life. Friends, family, and job demands may all mount up. When you combine it with the added stress and strains of contemporary life, it's easy to get disoriented and look for a way out.

Rather than stumbling around in the dark, you must learn to eliminate the emotional clutter from your life. When you let go of the things that no longer serve you and reconnect with the heart of who you are, you may experience some incredibly profound internal shifts that result in increased strength and pleasure.

Allow yourself to let go of the extremes and take steps to reconnect with your true self. Begin to separate from those that impede your overall quality of life by simplifying your thoughts and enjoyment. We weren't created on this earth to be burdened by the suffering and instability of others. Take charge of your destiny and resist the urge to impress others.

Signs you're dealing with emotional build-up.
Feeling adrift at sea, with no sense of direction or purpose? Do you have bad coping and numbing practices that further hurt your family and home life? These are all symptoms that you're struggling with emotional congestion.

Going from extremes

Take a moment to analyze your emotions. What is your current emotional temperature? If you're always "frazzled" or tense, your emotional or mental headspace could be clogged with things that shouldn't be there. Mood swings are a typical technique for our mind to educate us or somehow raise the warning cry that something isn't right, and they're often the first sign that something isn't right.

Losing who you are

What stage of life are you at right now? Could you express the essence of who you are in 5 seconds if someone asked you? Many of us are completely unaware of who we are. As a result, we don't know what we want out of our lives, relationships, or careers. When you've lost sight of who you are and what you want, even the essentials seem elusive. You're bumbling around in the dark, unsure of where you're going.

It never gets better.

When we have the guts to pay attention to our feelings, they provide a wealth of information. If you're feeling hopeless or entirely disappointed, it's because your emotions are warning you that you're on the wrong track. It's not natural to be unhappy in your relationships, friendships, where you live, where you work, and so on. It's also unhealthy to have negative ideas, attitudes, outlooks, or behaviors all of the time.

Questioning the core

Do you find yourself second-guessing everything you do? Or every decision you make? Questioning is a subtle method of pointing out problems in the life we're creating. When we doubt ourselves, it's usually because we're aware that the decisions we're making are incorrect or because we believe we're drifting further away from the things that bring us joy.

Numbing behavior

Promiscuity, alcoholism, gambling, and drug use can all be symptoms that you're avoiding dealing with underlying difficulties in your life. When we're dissatisfied, we'll go to any length to hide our feelings. This involves suppressing the pain and diverting our attention away through harmful behavior and relationships that jeopardize our long-term well-being.

Complete disconnection

Do you feel utterly cut off from the life you've created and the people you've surrounded yourself with? Feeling that you and your partner have lost touch or that you've chosen the incorrect job path? Total separation from your life is typically a sign that you've been constructing someone else's castle. During these moments, it's time to take a step back and reflect on who you are at your core and what you want in life.

Where all the clutter comes from.

Clutter does not appear anywhere. Faced with the stress and pressures of our friends, family, and even the ongoing anguish of our past, we accumulate emotional, spiritual, and mental clutter.

You've lost track of yourself.

It's all too easy to become overwhelmed by life's and our professions' responsibilities. The more responsibilities you take on, the simpler it becomes to give up small bits of yourself... until you find yourself at a fork in the road with a stranger and no idea which way to go. To live happy lives, we must first understand who we are and then fearlessly pursue our goals.

Running from the pain.

The nonstop marathon we run to escape our suffering is one of the most prevalent reasons we find ourselves living in a crowded mental nightmare. Our previous traumas continue to harm us, so we try everything we can to bury those emotions and forget about them. However, no matter how many "things" we hide them under, they don't disappear.

Over-reliance on the familiar

Contrary to popular belief, getting too comfortable (in a relationship or even a family) isn't a good thing. When we become too comfortable, we lose sight of our skills and interests, which give us our distinct flavor. The more you lean on the familiar for comfort, the more you'll find yourself accumulating other people's baggage in your life. There's a risk of being on autopilot when it comes to life.

The compulsive need to over-function

Those who have a crowded emotional headspace frequently feel compelled to over-function. This stems from a need to prove oneself in the face of their fears, as well as a desire to "belong." In fact, all of this is really a diversion; they're trying to avoid the agony of their past and the genuine emotions that are consuming them at their core.

Looking for a savior

We are the only ones with the ability to steer or change the direction of our life. On the other hand, failure to recognize this will put you in the trenches, seeking a rescue. You lose sight of yourself because you cannot see your abilities until there is nothing of worth left. You vanish, expecting someone to perform something that only you could have done all along.

Need-to-please

Do you feel compelled to satisfy others, whether family, coworkers, or even strangers? The more you give of yourself in service of others, the more likely you are to lose sight of yourself. It's a delicate balance to strike, but keep in mind that your personal needs are just as vital as anybody else's.

Common Types of Emotional Clutter

Emotional clutter is a topic that is rarely discussed. It's simpler to concentrate on the tangible stuff in our houses. However, because the emotions we hang on influence every aspect of our lives, it's critical to discuss emotional clutter.

Emotional clutter can be difficult to deal with. Every individual has had a distinct life experience. Recognizing our ideas and feelings requires self-awareness before we can move through them.

Many of these feelings manifest themselves in your house as physical clutter. Decide to let go of emotional baggage to transform your viewpoint and enhance your life.

It's okay to experience unpleasant feelings. They are an inevitable part of being alive and being able to feel. We must neither deny nor dismiss them. But we also don't want to be trapped thinking about them all the time.

The most prevalent sorts of emotional clutter we have are listed below.

Fear & anxiety

Anxiety and fear may paralyze you. Because we don't enjoy being uncomfortable, it's natural to avoid pushing limits or venturing outside of our comfort zones.

The finest things in life are frequently found on the other side of your anxieties.

We become trapped when we don't allow ourselves to work through and overcome our concerns.

I knew I'd be pushed past my comfort zone when I started my author journey, and I was correct! I learned to accept discomfort as a part of life. I even found myself enjoying it. That doesn't mean I appreciate it, but I recognize that it is the only way to progress.

Your objectives should be significant enough to you that they force you to face your concerns. You have to be so desperate for whatever it is that you're prepared to put up with it. Perhaps your objective is to improve your connection. Being open and honest might be frightening, but the benefits of doing so outweigh the risks.

When dread manifests itself in the form of physical clutter. Fear and worry may manifest themselves in the form of physical clutter. One of the reasons you hold on to clutter is fear. You may be concerned that you may want the item again in the future or that you will regret getting rid of it. You must desire all of the benefits of a clutter-free house more than your fear of letting go.

Guilt & shame

It's difficult to let go of the past. When we think back on our mistakes, we may feel guilty or ashamed. Neither of these feelings is beneficial. They make us feel worthless and only seek to drag us down.

Obsessing over the past does nothing. Instead, it degrades the present. Choose to let go of previous mistakes and concentrate on making better choices in the future.

Don't stake your reputation on what you did. You can modify it.

Filling up our calendars is another way guilt manifests. We feel bad about saying no, so we overcommit and attempt to be all things to all people. Burnout is a common result of this.

When remorse manifests itself in the form of physical clutter. When we get things we don't desire, our shame manifests as physical clutter. Recognize that the gift was given to benefit your life. If not, it's clutter, and it's time to get rid of it. People who care about you don't want you to feel guilty about keeping presents.

Anger & bitterness

Anger is a challenging emotion. The reasons we are upset are frequently justified, yet staying on with our rage, even if justifiable, causes us more harm in the long run.

It's much too short a life to waste being angry and resentful. When you decide to let things go, your life will suddenly improve.

It isn't a question of whether or not the person with whom you are furious and resentful deserves it.

It's all about letting go of emotional baggage so you may be your healthiest and happiest self.

Regret

Guilt and humiliation have certain parallels with regret. It's frequently linked to refusing to let go of past decisions. We lament the fact that we failed at anything or that we never attempted. We wish we could go back in time and do things differently.

You might be able to modify things in certain circumstances. Maybe there's still time to try something new or make apologies. However, even if it isn't, you may still choose to let it go.

Regret only serves to drag you down. The best thing you can do is learn from your mistakes, put the past behind you, and move on.

When remorse becomes a physical blight.
When you cling to expensive products you don't use because you spent so much money on them, regret might manifest as physical clutter.

Maybe you believed you'd put it to good use. It appeared to enhance your life, but it did not. Then, you find it difficult to let go because of the money you spent. But here's the thing: Regardless, the funds have already been spent.

Don't keep a tangible memento of your bad decisions to remind yourself of them.

Choose to forget about the blunder and focus on the lesson. Don't cling to your regrets.

Denial

Denial is a difficult emotion to get past since it requires you to see it work through it, and denial is all about pretending it isn't occurring.

Accepting life as it is might be difficult. However, you can't work on something you refuse to accept.

You'll never be content if you spend your entire life blaming others and acting like a victim. You'll feel powerless.

Because you can't influence anyone else, the most important thing you can do is identify and adjust your own role in your life.

Don't try to conceal your limitations or circumstances. Each of us has the same number of hours in a day: 24. Accept the reality.

When denial manifests itself in physical clutter.
When we maintain belongings from our past that have no relevance in our current lives, denial manifests itself as physical clutter. We preserve clothing that no longer fit from before we had children. Perhaps we'll save furnishings for when we move into a larger home.

We save things for a life we wish we had rather than the one we have now.

Recognize and accept your current situation in life. Self-awareness is the first step towards taking responsibility for your actions. Be honest with yourself, and don't pretend you don't know the truth.

Sadness

It's difficult to clear off sadness. It's quite difficult. It's not always simple to let go when life throws you a curveball. There is a time for sorrow, and not everything sad can be ignored.

When you've lost a loved one, you may constantly feel sorrowful. It's not something you can just forget about. And it's okay when the only thing you can do is take the next small step.

Working out your feelings and ideas with a trustworthy friend or counselor may be really helpful.

In other circumstances, grief is linked to a refusal to let go of the past. We may be disappointed by missed chances or shattered relationships. We don't seem to be able to let go of our hurt and despair.

When melancholy manifests itself in the form of physical clutter.

Sadness may be a motivator for clinging to things. Perhaps a significant figure in your life passed away. You may be clinging to their belongings because you have a sentimental relationship with them and find it difficult to let go.

The experiences you shared with that individual will be remembered for a long time. To remember someone well, you don't need to keep their stuff.

Clutter frequently appears in acute situations of melancholy that have developed into depression. Depression and clutter have been linked in studies.

Discouragement & self-doubt

Life is unpredictable. It's all too simple to get down on yourself and start believing things about yourself that aren't true.

Make no comparisons to others. Discontent and envy may flourish on social media. Identify the falsehoods that are running through your mind. Substitute the truth for them.

You are deserving. You are sufficient.

Our ideas impose limitations on us. We will live tiny if we question ourselves and think small. Never let your limiting beliefs rule your actions.

Allow yourself to have huge dreams. Believe in yourself and your abilities.

Overwhelmed & indecisive

Overwhelm, like fear, can halt our progress. Many people's first instinct when they are overwhelmed is to do nothing. It prevents you from moving forward or acting.

You may feel undecided when you're overloaded. Stress makes it difficult to make decisions, at the very least, not good ones.

You may feel overwhelmed by your life as a whole because your calendar is too full. It might be daunting when we don't have enough margin and rush from one item to the next. Protect your schedule to avoid feeling overwhelmed.

When anxiety manifests as physical clutter.

We shut off when we are too overwhelmed to cope with the physical clutter. Create a strategy and take little measures to counteract this. Start with tiny decisions and work your way up to bigger ones if you're having trouble being decisive.

Benefits of letting go of emotional clutter

Considering what we've all been there, we might benefit from a mental and emotional decluttering of our thoughts and feelings. Recognize the power of letting go and opening up to gain a better feeling of serenity and clarity.

Increased concentration

Decluttering our emotional baggage is so therapeutic that it clears our mental space, which helps with focus and decision-making. Like our lives and houses, our brains have a restricted amount of room. Allowing ourselves to let go of the negative and poisonous allows us to focus on the positive aspects of our nature and cognitive talents.

Greater sense of peace

When you finally start letting go of the negative things and people in your life, you'll feel an immediate sense of serenity and tranquility. Your neurosis may subside, and you may sleep better. You could even discover that you have more energy during the day or for activities you used to like. Decluttering our emotional life brings a profound sense of calm.

Releasing the past

While the past may be a valuable lesson, emotionally clinging to it is poisonous and self-defeating. It is impossible to change the past. Now, we can only try to avoid it from happening again. When you learn to separate yourself from negativity, you'll realize that you can take the lessons you need from the past and bury them where it belongs. It's impossible to change, yet it's already altered you. Allow it to go.

Boosting your emotions

Getting rid of the toxic garbage in your life may provide your emotions and emotional health a significant boost. Many of our mood swings and outbursts are unspoken expressions of issues we aren't confronting. We liberate ourselves to be joyful when we eventually take a deep breath and boldly tackle these bad parts of ourselves and our lives.

Focusing on what matters

Your life and mind will have more room for the things that are important if you get rid of all the "junk." Consider those who love and support you, as well as more financially gratifying and meaningful work prospects. Our ethereal life has a certain amount of space, and it's up to us to fill it with only what provides us significance and joy during our time on this earth.

Letting go of emotional clutter

Keeping your feelings bottled up might make you feel stuck in the past. However, you may channel that suppressed energy into a more pleasant existence by resolving these sentiments.

We must regularly deal with our emotions and get rid of the useless anxieties that plague our brains. This is known as "emotional decluttering," and it's a fantastic method to clear your head. Anxiety and despair typically follow when emotions are suppressed. Therefore, it's critical to clear out your ideas for a fresh start.

Consider unresolved difficulties as trapped energy that prevents us from living a better, more fulfilling life. We will have more energy to build the life we want if we spend more time working on ourselves, allowing ourselves to feel, and then letting go of bad feelings.

You don't have to be lost in emotional clutter for the rest of your life. Simple tactics like simplifying, chasing your pleasure, and disconnecting from things that no longer serve you can help you reclaim your inner joy, happiness, and satisfaction.

Simplify things

The first step in emotionally decluttering your life is to simplify things and streamline how you deal with emotions. That includes looking at your life and the things that cause you tension, pain, or any other form of dissatisfaction. Then take the necessary steps to eliminate those items from your gravitation and simplify your life.

Reduce the activities, pastimes, and people in your life that hinder rather than enhance your quality of life. Look for individuals and situations that make you feel stressed, and utilize them to bomb your day whenever you come across them.

Ensure your life isn't any more complicated than it has to be. You don't have to keep a relationship with someone who isn't kind to you, who exploits you, or who goes out of their way to hurt you. Stop wasting time on frivolous things that irritate you and start delving deeper into what you truly desire from life and yourself. Then you may start advocating for what you truly desire.

Master the art of saying "no."

If we genuinely want to live a life of our design, we must become comfortable with the word "no" and begin incorporating it into our daily lives. Words that begin with "no" aren't necessarily negative. It's a protective term, and it may help us feel safe and powerful about who we are and what we want.

Many individuals struggle with saying no to things they don't have time for or don't want to do. Even so, it's one of the most crucial life skills we can learn. It's not impolite to say no to something you don't feel prepared to handle; it's self-care and a sign of strength.

If you learn to say no, your perspectives will shift dramatically, and you'll soon see "no" as a positive rather than a negative. Turning down things that aren't right for us makes us stronger and our lives more lovely for the experience. A world ruled by "yes" is a world ruled by tiredness. Say "no" when it's convenient for you, and you'll receive the time and space you require when you need it.

Pursue your joy

A crowded existence is oppressive, preventing us from perceiving our natural route to satisfaction. The more room we devote to distractions and numbing practices, the more distant we grow from our natural feeling of delight. If you can't seem to find contentment in the thick of it all, take a step back and look within.

Rekindle your loves and activities that make your heart sing. Rekindle your passions and rediscover the things that make your life exciting and intriguing once again.

Pursue your delight and recognize that you, like everyone else in the world, have a right to genuine happiness. For a little while, stop sacrificing yourself on the altar of someone else's needs and focus on your own. Follow your dreams for the life you want to live and the future you want to build. No one can provide you with it. You must construct it for yourself.

Thin out your friend list

We only have so much space in our lives for relationships; filling it with individuals who drain our energy and make us feel small detract from our overall quality of life. Reduce your buddy list and quit wasting time with people that deplete you or force you to go places you don't want to go.

People that make us furious, sad, or make us feel insignificant should be avoided at all costs. Remove individuals from your timeline who provide more negativity than positivity.

Only hang out with individuals that make you feel good or who encourage you to be a better person than you were yesterday. Nobody owes you their time, energy, money, or space. By narrowing down your buddy list, you may stand up for yourself and find a new layer of tranquility.

Increase your time in the real world

If you've been avoiding the agony and misery of your ill-fitting existence for a long time, chances are you haven't been present in a long time. Being present is difficult because it requires us to confront our emotions and our decisions. It's fully present in our bodies and feeling fully present in our sentiments.

Learn to value being present in the moment and recognize the rewards this presence may provide. Pay notice to everything that your body is attempting to say to you. Pay heed to your feelings. Which of your decisions and the people around you is attempting to teach you?

Reduce the amount of time you spend on social media and the time you spend diverting yourself or "getting lost."

Stop comparing yourself to others and realize that everyone has their unique journey to pursue throughout their time here. Stop hurrying for the future or fleeing from the past and instead embrace the present. Simply be present at the moment and enjoy things as they are. After all, you're never going to be in this situation again.

Take your emotional temperature.

It's uncomfortable to sit with our emotions, but they have a purpose and must be acknowledged. We should take our emotional temps regularly and utilize this procedure to know our emotions and how they affect us.

Start accepting your emotions and getting in the habit of addressing them head-on instead of hiding them deep down till they rot. Learn to be at ease with your emotions and cherish them for what they can contribute to your life.

Try start by dedicating a few minutes each day to this exercise. Get a journal and find a quiet spot to write for 10–15 minutes. Shut your eyes and take a couple of full breaths. Concentrate on your body and pay attention to your emotions. Make a list of any feelings you experience, as well as any reactions they elicit.

Become a master of moving on

If you genuinely want to transcend all of the trash and anguish that is holding you back, you must learn the art of moving on. That includes letting go of the past and emotionally distancing yourself from things that harm you but are out of your control.

Stop clinging to things that don't serve you anymore. Stop trying to live up to other people's expectations and start following your own. Remove yourself from those who make you feel insignificant.

Move on from the situations and past injuries that continue to hurt you with no end in sight. We define our expectations for how we want to be treated and how we want to feel. Stop allowing the useless things to hold you back from greatness and learn to master the art of moving on.

Having to be the perfect something. (Know it?).

We'll be so adept at what we do that, some days, it'll frighten us. On other days, we'll be a complete disaster. Every day, though, we'll be sufficient. It's exhausting to have to be the perfect partner/parent/colleague/employee (uggghh - I'm exhausted just listing them). And it's unthinkable. You'll be further away from perfection in one role while you go closer to perfection in another. Whatever you are is enough, so try on different roles to see what fits, take a step sideways, and be willing to make mistakes. Be the most human version of yourself. They're a lot more enjoyable to be around than the flawless people.

People-clutter.

One-sided friendships. Toxic relationships. People who deplete, fade, or diminish you. Draw a big, heavy underline between you and them when you can, and utilize the space they're making up for the people you want to be with. Jim Rohn, a motivational speaker, has stated that we become the average of the five people with whom we spend the most time with. It's logical. We open up to those we let into our lives. We become vulnerable to their affection, knowledge, warmth, influence, and opinions - particularly their opinion of us. When we allow ourselves to be open to the good, we also allow ourselves to the negative. It's just how things are. In five words, how would you describe each of your five people? If the comments you're hearing are hurtful, consider what you're receiving out of the connection. It's just not good for you if it's not good for you. Fullstop. It's not always about you or them, but rather the mix of the two of you.

The thing about not making a decision ...

It is still a decision to keep still if you do not decide. This is good for a while, even wise, but if you continue to do nothing, it will soon hold you down. Things are possible, and doing nothing is worse than doing it wrong. At the very least, if you try something and it doesn't work out, you can go on, whereas the 'what ifs' of inaction would keep you rooted in place indefinitely. A leap of faith is sometimes the only way ahead. Holding oneself back from moving uses up mental and emotional energy. What are some of the items you're delaying deciding on? Make a deadline for yourself and go for it. What's keeping you from letting it go if that's the case?

The drama. Oh, the drama!

Not the lighthearted sort that comes with commercial breaks, but the kind that will drive you insane if you allow it. This includes everything from voicemails, texts, emails, and more, all of which make you feel bad whenever you go there. Does someone or something in your life always bring you down?

The delete key was created precisely to free us from the grip of fools in our life. It's simple to use. That is exactly what it is for.

The reasons not to.

Even if there are valid reasons for not starting a relationship, making a career shift, applying for a new job, or taking a vacation or adventure, there will always be excuses for not doing so. It'll never feel more terrifying than when you're on the verge of deciding whether to go or stay, yet fear can be a filthy little liar and disguise itself as a stop sign. It's not the case. It's a sign that you're about to embark on a very courageous endeavor. Take a chance on it. Just take one modest step over the line and let the momentum carry you the rest of the way. Make the phone, send the email, start the discussion, utter the words – and watch the doors open.

1. Yes. That.

It's very simple to fall into the snare of contrasting ourselves with others. (Oh, I recognize this one!) You never know what goes on behind the scenes or what it feels like to walk in someone else's shoes. If you're still on your journey, be focused, and don't get distracted by the fact that someone is ahead of you on the path. They may appear to be more successful, happier, wealthier, kinder, or powerful from the outside. However, keep going. You can be all of these things. There's no reason why you can't be more.

Avoidance.

It's natural to avoid things out of dread of what could happen if you do them, yet avoiding essential things has its own set of repercussions. Difficult situations do not disappear just because they are ignored. It would be nice to heed the warning, but it isn't how they usually operate. Be bold, turn around, and face the world. If you don't do it, you won't be able to go on to anything greater.

Thoughts to fly by or fall by.

The finest things in life start with a thought and may end with one too. Thoughts have tremendous power, yet they are just that - thoughts. Carefully select those to whom you delegate authority. You'll be able to take off if you choose the appropriate ones. You'll be grounded if you choose the incorrect ones. You'll face-plant into the runway if you choose the incorrect ones. Take your time. It's entirely in your control.

The items are supposed to make you feel attractive while you're around them. But they aren't.

Anything that makes you feel overweight, unattractive, frumpy, ignorant, or inferior has no place in your life. People, periodicals, television shows, books, boyfriends, friends, partners, and family are just a few examples. They're horrible to have around if they make you feel lousy.

Oh, wait. No, they're not.

A particular type of 'people clutter.' They're the 'friends' who make you feel bad about yourself. Never show up on time, want to be on call, give you backhanded compliments as though you're the keeper of unpleasant things to say to others, and constantly boast about how great they are while overlooking that you're doing just fine. They're your worst nightmares.

They're poisonous takers and take up valuable real estate. They should be moved on.

I'm aware that we've reached the end of our conversation. I truly believe that. But I'm going to keep this... because... because...

Anything that keeps you reminiscing and feeling unhappy isn't good for you. I'm referring to the folks (as in exes) you keep in touch with. You may convince yourself that everything is OK, that you're still friends, that you're capable of handling it – blah blah blah – but it's more likely that it will turn out to be a stunning act of self-sabotage. You'll probably keep checking (secretly – who wouldn't?) to make sure there's no one new, or that if there is, they don't appear to be as happy with them as they were with you. You know where this is going, and it's not going to be pleasant. Simply said, quit. Allow them to leave. Unfriend and unfollow each other. Unlike. It's unnecessary clutter, and there's nothing there for you.

In the gene pool, there is no protective barrier.

You don't have to spend time with someone just because you share genetics with them. If you feel 'less than' while you're around them, it's a good idea to keep your distance. Nobody claimed genes were good at determining connections, but if you want to be, they are. You don't have to like your biological relatives. Not even a smidgeon. Don't be a doormat, but be accepting and compassionate. We are raised with specific messages from our families, and since those messages have been there for a long time – as in, "for our whole lives" - we tend to swallow them whole without questioning their meaning. Chew them up to get a sense of how they taste, then swallow or spit them out. Nobody said you had to agree with, like, or spend time with them simply because you share DNA.

Memories aren't the same as facts. (Though they'll make you believe otherwise.)

The thing with memories is this: They aren't always as accurate as they claim to be. Our memories are shaped by what we pay attention to and how we interpret events, which we determine. When we're happy, we notice joyful things and use a positive filter to transform occurrences into memories. We search for evidence to back up our beliefs and pay less attention to contradictions. When we're in a bad mood, we do the same thing. Let me give you an illustration. If you're having trouble believing that you're not good at relationships because they constantly seem to end (or because one has just ended), you'll filter through memories (automatically and unconsciously) and keep the ones that fit how you're feeling. They'll likely be ones where you've been wounded or disappointed, but you won't remember the recollections of successful relationships or those involved who liked being with you. Let go of the notion that your recollections are correct and understand the difference between them and the facts. The most suffocating type of clutter is inaccurate recollections.

The requirement for permission.

You don't have to have everyone's love and approval. Some will adore you, some will think little of you, and others will think nothing of you at all. There will always be critics. It's only that it's currently up to your portion of the planet. Keep the ones that love you (as long as it's not long-distance love), learn from the ones who don't, and move on. Other than that, you're wasting your time and making things more difficult.

Over and over again, I'm thinking about the same thing, and... (Really, it's not going to change.) It's just not the case.)

Who hasn't thought about something repeatedly to feel better about it? There comes the point where repeating something that makes you feel unpleasant is detrimental to your health. It's known as rumination, and it's linked to depression. There are times when there are no answers. If they haven't presented themselves to you yet, going over it again is unlikely to pull them out into the open. With regards to change, there are many elements at play. However, it is more vital to be receptive to new ideas and individuals rather than forcing anything different to happen. There will be periods in our lives when we feel stripped bare, but this sensation will not last. We'll eventually rebuild in ways we couldn't have dreamed, but only after the what-ifs, maybes, shoulds, and other restricting beliefs have been removed from our minds.

I'm waiting for everything to come together.

In actuality, there is no beginning, middle, or end. (Pity.) Why's it easy to put off moving ahead (for example, from a broken relationship) until things make sense ('but I don't see it - we were just so happy). The trouble is that many times the one thing that will make everything make sense hasn't happened yet, and won't until you let go of the clutter and go forward. Consider the times in your life when things didn't make sense.

By now (depending on how far back in time you've gone), the chances are that they have contributed to your current situation even in the tiniest way. Things will ultimately make sense. Wait for the parts to fall into place. I can see how the relationships that didn't work out prepared me for those that did. There have also been times when I applied for jobs and didn't receive them, which seemed awful at the moment but opened the door for bigger options.

Imagine the life you want to lead.

Consider your ideal existence to empower yourself. Would it entail a professional shift, pursuing a hobby, or contributing to society somehow? By visualizing where you want to go, you may begin to consider the measures required to get there.

Make a list of how your life is right now.

Make a list of everything that matters to you right now: your friends, your work, your love life, and anything else. When considering a life change, pay attention to how you feel about these things. Which areas do you believe you should focus on?

For instance, to zero in on your adoration life yet realize you haven't continued from your ex-accomplice, here you'll have to relinquish your sentiments.

List the things limiting you.

Make a list of all the circumstances or places you need to handle based on the steps above. These are the things that are preventing or restricting your progress.

This phase is critical for emotional decluttering. You need to go deep and figure out where you're stuck. Putting ideas down in writing makes it easier to see the big picture – and the work that must be done.

Revisit these scenarios & Emotions

After you've figured out what's keeping you from going forward, go through each situation and fully feel those feelings.

If it's about an ex-partner you're still not over, get yourself a cup of tea and reflect on how they made you feel during and after the relationship. We often suppress our emotions, distracting ourselves with food, booze, or anything else that will dull the pain. The key is to let go of the suppressed feeling.

You sweep away these blockages and limitations with a mental broom once you start addressing these emotions and purging. Simply put pen to paper and allow your stream of consciousness to dictate what it needs.

Bleeding out through a 'bad' situation.

When you frame things like a poor circumstance, you risk losing confidence and motivation. Things aren't necessarily awful just because they aren't good. Everything we go through molds us, but it is up to us whether that molding is for the better or the worst. It's critical not to let your self-esteem, motivation, or confidence slip through the gaps of a negative scenario. We have the option of becoming victims of our circumstances or taking control of our responses. We don't always control what happens to us, but everything provides a chance to grow as a person: to be braver, stronger, smarter, kinder, and more resilient. Of course, it's perfectly OK to fall apart first. It might feel like the only option at times. But, when you're ready to, make sure you stand right back up.

Believing that a successful relationship must endure indefinitely.

Love, learning, and development are all characteristics of a successful partnership. Growth can halt for at least one person in a pair, and the relationship, as well as the individuals in it, might stall – but it doesn't imply the relationship hasn't been a success. Every relationship reaches a make-or-break stage at some point. This is the moment in some partnerships where it's time to fight. When you're both 'in,' don't see the battle as a sign that things are about to end; instead, see it as a sign that you're about to enter a new stage of your relationship—knowing when the time up requires a lot of guts. We undervalue the extent to which we evolve. People will be different ten years from now than ten years ago. Relationships, occupations, and other aspects of our history may no longer match who we are as a result. They may develop with us at times. They don't always work. That isn't to say they weren't significant, successful, or incredible to be a part of at the time. It may be excruciatingly difficult to hold on when there is nothing left to hold on to. It's all right to let go on sometimes. It's sometimes the only option left.

Get support

Working with emotional clutter necessitates seeking assistance and support. If you've been harboring these feelings for a long time, it's a good idea to get professional treatment.

Have supporting friends or family members in your life. Having someone you care about and trust at your side might help you work through tough habits and feelings.

Create new habits

Decide to stop dwelling on your unpleasant feelings. Don't succumb to self-destructive actions or patterns. Instead, decide to establish new behaviors. Change your viewpoint by focusing on appreciation.

It's fine if not every day is intended to be sunshine and flowers. That is something we can and should be open about. You develop emotional clutter when you bottle up your sentiments.

When those sensations arise, do something that will give you life. Read a book, write in a diary, chat with a friend, or go for a walk. Self-care is important, as is dealing with your emotions.

Dealing with emotional clutter might be more difficult than dealing with physical clutter. It goes unnoticed and is frequently overlooked. Processing sentiments takes time, especially if you've been holding them for a long period. However, as you go through your feelings, you will feel lighter.

Continue to take one step at a time to get to a better, baggage-free state. By letting go of the past, you may create a better life for yourself.

Tell yourself a new, empowering story.

Take the time to compose your new tale of how you want your life to look once you've addressed the emotions that were holding you back. You are your own dearest companion and backer; consequently, put your confidence in yourself to distinguish your drawn-out objectives. With a clearer mind, you'll notice that the energy you used to generate negative ideas may now be put to better use.

Take tiny, everyday efforts toward the new tale to help it become a reality - no matter how little they may appear. Working on the story regularly will instill confidence in you. Be kind to yourself along the journey. In the end, you will succeed, even if it takes a long time now.

How to let go of Fear & anxiety

Fear is one of the most powerful negative emotions that might diminish your ability to attract what you want.

When you consider all that may go wrong in life, do you get apprehensive, agitated, or scared?

If that's the case, you're not alone! You will, however, need to devise a strategy for shifting this perspective.

Fear holds you back and keeps you focused on the thought of lack, but love fills you with happiness and raises your energy level, allowing you to manifest more effectively.

Understand Your Fears

To begin, examine your concerns and determine the source of your discontent.

This isn't a simple procedure. It may be extremely frightening. But it pays off.

1. Embrace and Control Your Feelings.
You must realize that changing fear into love does not imply suppressing or ignoring your feelings.

Learning to let go through conquering your emotions is a beneficial skill in this situation; the idea is that you can completely accept those feelings, recognize them, and find a method to process them so that they may be released.

Write them down in a notebook, express them via art (painting or music), or channel them into physical activities like jogging, horseback riding, dancing, or boxing.

2. Write Down Your Fears.
Because you'll be focused on your worries, this may seem paradoxical.

However, acknowledging your troubles is sometimes necessary to let them go.

Sit down and write out the things bothering you.

When you put your anxieties on paper, you'll notice that they're silly, and it'll be easier to forget about them.

On the other side, you may discover worries that you were previously unaware of. Don't worry; everything is OK.

Many of us have internal concerns that are eating us alive, but we've had them for so long that they've become subconscious beliefs that we're unaware of.

So, after you've discovered your buried worries, you can begin the process of letting them go.

3. Demystify Your Fears

Fear's potency stems partly from the fact that it is frequently misunderstood. Consider occasions when you've had a creeping disquiet, a thumping heart, or a dread of failure without truly understanding what's frightening you or why.

Seek to comprehend fear to make more room for love and lessen the power of dread.

Look it in the eyes and try to figure out where it came from, what it means, how it links to your self-image, and so on.

In many situations, you'll discover the kinds of limiting beliefs that prevent individuals from correctly applying the Law of Attraction.

You may also replace such beliefs with positive, loving ones by using tools like affirmations and a concentration wheel.

Work On Letting Go Of Your Fears

You may begin removing your anxieties from your life now that they are no longer hidden.

You become aware of your predicament, and now you can permanently alter your relationship with fear. Here are a few tips to help you deal with fear freshly and excitingly.

1. Focus On Doing Good

By the day's end, we as a whole need to be heard, regarded, and seen.

As a result, simply sitting with another person and listening to what they have to say is one of the most significant actions you can do.

Empathize with them, try to comprehend their situation, and be present.

This sort of love transforms the other person's life and fills you with compassion; the next time you're afraid, consider how you may show love in this way and direct your attention toward doing so.

2. Associate Your Transformation With A Special Object.
You can assign something similar to the associated aim of converting fear into love, just as you can have one specific object that you tie to your Law of Attraction goals.

A little rock or stone, which you can hold in your palm and imagine anxiety flowing into it and love pouring back out of it, soaking into your flesh, is a popular choice here.

Other suggestions include a piece of jewelry (such as a heart necklace or a rose quartz ring) that you may wear whenever you need a reminder to focus on love or a candle with a smell that makes you feel calm and solid.

3. Stay Open
Even if you're generally an outgoing person, it's natural to shut down at moments of dread.

When fear begins to paralyze you, you'll struggle to keep your mind and heart open to alternative options.

Consider how you might feel better in your present position, remove unassuming, however purposeful strides from your usual range of familiarity, and permit others to take care of you when they need to (rather than driving them away).

Don't isolate yourself or keep all of your problems concealed; reach out to your friends and family, and realize that it's okay to be vulnerable.

4. Radiate Love

As previously mentioned, one method to radiate love is to demonstrate compassion and understanding to others around you. It isn't, however, the sole option. For example, you might practice meditation by envisioning your heart spreading love to others, whether it's a community in need, an individual who is grieving, or just someone you always hope the best for.

This simple act puts you in touch with plenty, putting you in the best position to materialize the future you desire. Consider the age-old concept of performing one random act of kindness every day.

As Law of Attraction specialists often point out, you attract what you send out into the world, and doing wonderful things for strangers and friends alike helps you attract a lot more kindness into your own life.

How to let go of Guilt & shame

What Makes Us Feel Guilty and Shameful?

In our lives, guilt and shame serve a vital role. Guilt is that nagging feeling you get before doing something you know is bad. Our conscience is guilty. Its goal is to warn us when we will do or are doing anything against our beliefs. As we get older, we all establish a set of values. Much of it is ingrained in us due to our upbringing and culture. Our value system is a collection of beliefs that govern our actions. We feel guilty when we will do or have done anything that goes against this value system. Guilt signals that we should take a break and try something new.

We feel shame when we reject our sentiments of remorse and continue to do what we perceive is wrong. When we internalize guilt and believe we are horrible because we did something wrong and ignored our emotions of remorse, we experience shame. The goal of shame is to make us feel so horrible that we strive to make up for our wrongdoings. The humiliation, on the other hand, might be overwhelming at times. We attempt to hide what we've done. When others find out about the wrongs we've done, we feel even more ashamed. Or we don't know how to make amends. We hide what we've done rather than doing something to set things right. We deceive ourselves and cover up our mistakes. Hiding our mistakes simply adds to our feelings of guilt and humiliation.

Guilt and humiliation spiral into a vicious cycle that looks like this. Something is wrong with us. We have a sense of guilt. We don't fix what's broken. We are ashamed. We tell lies and try to hide what we've done. We have a greater sense of remorse and humiliation. This loop keeps repeating itself.

Letting go of Guilt and Shame

Face our wrongs – Remember that trying to hide our wrongdoings leads to a vicious cycle of guilt and humiliation. One method to break out from the pattern is to accept responsibility for our actions. Accepting responsibility for our mistakes is an essential element of evolving and growing as an individual. Admitting that you've made a mistake or done something wrong breaks the pattern and sets us free from our prison of guilt and shame. By verbalizing what you've done and preparing yourself to bear the consequences, you can face your mistakes and accept responsibility. Accepting responsibility for one's actions entails accepting the consequences of one's actions. It enables us to proceed to the next stage.

Make amends: Finding a means to make amends for what you›ve done can assist in breaking the pattern. We can›t always remedy a mistake directly. Certain things can›t be rectified. However, you can always do something nice for someone you›ve wronged or something beneficial for society as a whole.

Requesting forgiveness: When someone forgives us for our wrongs, we›ll feel a lot less guilty and ashamed. However, we must remember that we are attempting to better ourselves by asking for forgiveness. Being a better person entails not asking for forgiveness selfishly when doing so might harm the person we want forgiveness from. People are often so upset by our deeds that they refuse to remember or forgive the person who has harmed them.

Forgiveness of ourselves: Whether or whether the person we have injured forgives us, guilt and shame may persist until we forgive ourselves for our actions. Forgiving oneself brings the healing process to a close and removes any remaining feelings of guilt or shame.

How Do We Face Our Wrongs?

Begin by mentally reliving each year of your addiction or life, recalling any experiences that trigger feelings of regret or shame.

- Make a list of everything you think you did incorrectly.
- Consider which of your values you violated when you did something bad.
- Consider who was harmed as a result of your conduct.
- Take into account both those who were directly and indirectly harmed.
- Reflect on why you did the incorrect thing.
- Consider what you may have done differently.

How to let go of Anger & bitterness

It's starting to happen again. It may creep up on you, but it moves swiftly. You're on the verge of being enraged.

Anger is uncontrollable energy that takes hold of us and causes us to do or say things we wouldn't ordinarily do or say.

Holding on to anger has negative physical and emotional consequences. Eventually, it will force you to react irrationally and impulsively, jeopardizing your personal and professional relationships.

You know what I'm talking about if you've ever said anything hurtful or screamed at someone and subsequently felt like a jerk. Do you, however, know how to let go of your anger?

Fortunately, learning to let go of anger and hurt is achievable.

Why Recurring Anger Can Be a Dangerous Habit

In several studies, anger and resentment have been found to be related to heart disease and hypertension. Anger physical drains our energies and can have long-term consequences.

It's crucial to understand why you were upset in the first place before you can begin the process of letting go of your anger. We utilize anger as a second-hand emotion (or substitute emotion) to avoid fear, vulnerability, or pain.

Many things might cause pain, such as physical or mental abuse from a parent or spouse. It wasn't only the situation that got you upset; your mental process also played a role.

Anger, assumptions, and perceptions of a situation might trigger memories, leading individuals to believe that someone is trying to harm them. These faulty thinking habits might jeopardize your relationships and cause you to be stressed out. While rage is a natural emotion that everyone experiences, it frequently manifests itself as undesirable and unreasonable.

You can learn how to let go of resentment.

The good news is that you can break your anger habit and learn to let go of resentment.

Chronic anger is a learned characteristic.

If you grew up in a violent family and were frequently the victim of someone else's furious conduct in the past, or if you were somehow rewarded for your anger, you may develop chronic anger.

Being conscious of your anger, preparing yourself to behave differently in the future, taking action by finding help to control your emotions, and then sustaining your new perspective are some methods to begin reversing these sentiments.

Strategies on How to Let Go of Anger

1. Recognize where your rage is coming from.
Recognize when you're upset and try to figure out the cause of it. Is the reason something you can influence or modify, or is it beyond your control? Is your rage being provoked by someone you'll never see again, such as a supermarket clerk or a restaurant server? Or are you enraged by a family member or a friend?

This is crucial to understand since the anger you experience while interacting with individuals close to you is a continuous engagement. Escape the situation, relax, restructure your ideas, or communicate your anger directly in a calm and suitable tone are the best tactics to use in these instances.

Another technique to figure out what's causing your rage is to take a step back and assess your life. Are you exactly where you intended to be at this point? You're likely frustrated because your life isn't living up to your expectations or because you're not living up to the expectations you think others have for you.

Unhealthy relationships and prior experiences frequently fuel anger. When one person is often vulnerable or triggered by a prior hurt in their relationship, anger might mask the suffering. If you can pinpoint a previous event that is still hurting your life, you must confront it head-on to let it go.

2. Practice relaxation techniques.
Simple relaxation techniques can aid in the relief of furious sentiments. If you use these tactics frequently, you will find it easy to use them when you sense anger rising. It's critical

to figure out which approaches work best to process your thoughts more clearly.

Many people, for example, use aromatherapy to relax. Essential oils are a terrific stress reliever and easily available relaxation technique, whether you use them in a bath or a diffuser. Another popular method is to listen to relaxing music. This might assist you in diverting your attention away from the current issue and refocusing your thoughts.

3. Take a brief time out.
It is critical to recognize when you should take a break. If you see yourself getting angry while doing something or talking to someone, simply excuse yourself. Require a couple of moments to gather your considerations before you go so you can relinquish the terrible sentiments. Before you talk, take some time to consider how you want to reply.

Taking a break will keep you from saying anything you'll later regret because you were angry. Assuming you really want to have some time off, pick a quiet and mitigating area. Consider some relaxation techniques, such as slow, deep breathing, and mindfulness activities, to help you relax at this time.

Consider what you'll say when you're ready to return to the issue after your fury has dissipated. If you're chatting with someone, say how much you appreciate their patience and how grateful you are for the opportunity to relax.

4. Get daily exercise.
Stress and anger can be effectively relieved by physical activity. Physical activity allows you to express your feelings, so taking a daily walk or run might help you relax in general. Exercise can

also help your body release endorphins, which will make you feel better and lower your stress levels naturally.

Finding a healthy pastime, such as exercise, will help you relax by keeping your mind engaged. An attempt maybe a couple of things until you find something you appreciate. This will motivate you to take a break from your routine while also boosting your self-esteem.

5. Find workable solutions.

Rather than focusing on the source of your rage, try to find a solution. Is your partner, for example, always late for dinner? Find a real solution instead of dealing with this drama on a nightly basis. Perhaps you and your partner might agree to dine on your own on certain evenings, or you can arrange meals for later in the evening to work around their schedule better.

You must acknowledge the things over which you have no control and accept that you cannot alter them. Knowing what you can manage can help you make the most use of your limited resources. You may use the time you squander worrying about and attempting to alter problems over which you have no control on things over which you do have control, allowing you to make progress.

6. Don't hold grudges.

Holding grudges is harmful to your health more than it is to the other person's. They not only sap your vitality, but they also poison your emotional condition.

Even if you have been truly insulted, as most people have, instead of behaving like a victim, attempt to empathize. Forgiving thoughts will help you feel more in control and minimize your physiological stress reaction, which will help you feel less angry.

7. Practice forgiveness.
Forgiveness can take many forms, but it usually entails making a conscious decision to let go of angry sentiments and ideas of vengeance. Once you've done this, your anger will stop draining your energy, and you'll be able to relax.

The act that caused you damage may remain with you forever, but forgiveness will liberate you from the grip of the incident or person who did you harm. You are not forgiving someone else for their sake when you forgive them. Instead, you're doing it to reclaim control of your life and move on. This does not imply that you are forgetting or absolving yourself of the detrimental activity, but it will provide you with some relief.

8. Own your anger.
Before your anger takes control of you, you must learn to control it. Recognize when you're furious and tell yourself that you'll be able to overcome it. Remember that the sensation will pass quickly, and it will only grow as severe as you let it.

Our emotions' logic does not always make sense. For example, if you were harmed as a child by a parent and are still angry and waiting for someone else to repair it for you as an adult, you will never get over it. You must accept responsibility for your anger and address it to go on. You are the only one who has power over your emotions.

9. Talk to a friend.
Contact a close buddy you know will offer you their undivided attention. Allow them to hear your rage and frustrations and

receive feedback. A good buddy might be able to help you reframe a situation and see it from a fresh perspective.

It also feels nice to let off steam. Setting some boundaries for your ranting could be a good idea. For instance, ask a buddy if you can chat for five minutes... and then give yourself only five minutes to rant. Pay attention to how often you repeat yourself; you'll probably notice that you frequently do it to emphasize a point. Set time limitations to help you stay on track, organize your thoughts, and focus on a solution.

10. Recite positive affirmations.

Anger that returns is a confirmation. Negative affirmations must be replaced with positive ones. You can choose to think in a manner that fosters a bad mental environment for yourself and others around you, or you can choose to think in a way that fosters a healthy mental environment for yourself and those around you.

Tell yourself that you are in charge and that no one has the power to make you feel inferior. If you're starting to get upset, doing so will help you calm down. Learn to practice both current and future affirmations so you can use this approach to both avoid and cope with anger when it arises.

11. Express yourself in a journal

Perhaps the most proficient strategy to communicate and comprehend your displeasure is to expound on it in a notepad. You may carefully process your thoughts by writing them down.

You'll have the control you need to assess your responses after identifying the fundamental reasons for your anger. By raising your self-awareness, writing about your anger can help you learn from it and take constructive action to protect yourself in the future.

Instead of writing down their feelings, some people choose to sketch or paint them. This is also a good way to keep a journal. To help yourself move on, draw what your rage seems like and creatively express yourself.

12. Change your environment.

You may sometimes become irritated by your local surroundings. You may begin to feel stuck. You may avoid this by making personal time a priority.

You may be more prone to become enraged due to factors in your surroundings. For example, if you frequently become irritable in the mornings when racing about trying to get everyone ready for the day, try to find a way to relieve this tension the night before so you may lessen your burden in the morning.

Alternatively, if you've had a bad relationship, stay away from anything that reminds you of the person who injured you. This includes refraining from visiting areas where you used to spend time together and from listening to music that reminds you of them. You may need to take different routes to work or school to avoid being reminded of this individual, and you may need to change your routine to prevent bad thoughts.

13. Become more self-aware.

Increasing your self-awareness can assist you in preventing your anger from manifesting. Developing the ability to pay attention to your mind and analyze some of your negative ideas is necessary for being aware of your incorrect beliefs. You may use your strategies to shift the dynamics that are going on in your head and causing your emotions after you understand what causes your rage.

The outcomes of your self-awareness activities can lead to a permanent shift if you can love yourself and avoid a victim mindset. Being self-aware may identify the fundamental ingredients or sensations that trigger your anger, such as fear or pain.

14. Laugh.
Can you recall a time when you found yourself laughing at something that made you angry? Because comedy is both therapeutic and inspiring, this moment can be transformative. You may gain control over something if you can laugh about it instead of allow it to have power over you.

How to let go of Regret

You're not alone if you're wondering how to let go of regret. It's easy to look back and think of all the things you could have done differently, especially after a year of such loss and upheaval. Whether your regrets are major—such as declining a scholarship in your final year of high school—or minor—such as saying something hurtful in a day-to-day interaction—figuring out how to learn from and then let go of regret is good.

"There are individuals who claim, 'I spend my life with no regrets,' but I believe if we dissect it a little bit, we'll see that pretty much everyone has [them]," says Neal Roese, Ph.D., a social psychologist, and professor of marketing at Northwestern University's Kellogg School of Management.

According to Dr. Roese, regret is a negative feeling based on counterfactual thinking. Counterfactual thinking entails looking back and concocting hypothetical situations to persuade ourselves that things could have turned out differently. Suppose you regret not putting more effort into your past relationship. In that case, regret may lead you to believe that your actions might have repaired everything, or you may conclude that you'll never find anybody else. Dr. Roese continues, "Our brains are incredibly adept at expanding on or inventing these alternate universes in which we might have done things differently." "And a lot of it is driven by our desires, wants, and needs." It's just a manifestation of our desire to get there."

Even while regrets are an inevitable aspect of life, they can outlast their use. Why? The desire to get there may be a catalyst for development and progress, but it can trap us in a downward spiral of negativity and despair. So, if you're having trouble letting go of regret, here are nine tiny steps you may take to put some distance between yourself and your regrets.

1. Make a list of the lessons you've learned and refer to it when you need a reminder.

People who declare "I don't have any regrets" aren't always in denial (though they might be). According to Robert Allan, Ph.D., L.M.F.T., an emotionally focused therapy trainer and assistant professor of marriage and family therapy at the University of Colorado, Denver, "there's a possibility they've been able to use their sense of regret to learn from their conduct." According to Dr. Roese, regret is an important aspect of goal-setting because it allows you to consider preventing a similar outcome in the future. If you're drowning in what you could've done or said, instead, make a list of what you've learned and how you've changed. You may also utilize the current moment to uncover the lesson if all you can see is how bad life is right now due to your disaster. Rather than thinking, "Oh, if only things were different right now," consider what the disappointment, anger, or regret you're experiencing is teaching you. It's impossible to go back and change the past, but you can learn a lot about yourself by examining your feelings.

2. Rethink your "best-case scenario."
Dr. Roese notes, "Regret focuses on what you could have done differently." The fact is that you have no way of knowing if things would have turned out differently if you had taken a different choice. If you're regretting not saving more money, for example, it's a good idea to avoid thinking that "everything would have been wonderful if I'd kept to a savings plan." Savings may be helpful right now, but other variables may have contributed to your current situation at the time. Even if it's not obvious now, a few parts of your life may have improved as a result of your extra spending. Dr. Roese proposes that instead of designing a scenario that overemphasizes optimistic thinking, you consider how an alternative option may have negatively influenced you.

"This is just another way of gaining context and perspective," Dr. Roese explains, adding that "there are other reasons why anyone moment might have gone worse if you tried a little bit harder," and that "even among the choices you regret, there's probably evidence that you've done something brilliant along the way." And, if you're having problems making a single wise decision in the middle of your remorse, recall the first tip: Perhaps this scenario arose to teach you a lesson before the stakes become any greater. There's still time to alter your mind if you're reading this.

3. Try to forgive yourself.

Regrets are a sign that you have personal standards for how you conduct your life, but Dr. Roese emphasizes that part of being a human is occasionally falling short of those goals. When this happens, you'll almost certainly have to forgive yourself.

No enchanted cure can help you have an improved outlook on anything you lament immediately, yet you might start to give up by handling and excusing yourself for any apparent affronts. If you need to forgive yourself, we have a few suggestions, but the first is to pretend you're talking to a buddy (instead of yourself). This might assist you in unlocking self-compassion and moving past regret.

4. Distract yourself by trying something new.

According to Dr. Roese, our regrets might turn into ruminations when we feel stuck in our current circumstances. Dr. Roese proposes attempting something fresh if the epidemic has you sitting at home pondering (and overthinking) about regrettable experiences. This does not have to be a dramatic situation. "The cure is to try new things and break out of your routine in some manner," Dr. Roese explains. Consider making an ordinary stroll into an experience by taking a new route or getting something you wouldn't normally order online. Breaking up monotony not only helps you avoid ruminations but also has another benefit: Small methods to surprise yourself and attempt new things, according to Dr. Allan, might help you "trust in your potential to learn and grow." And when you feel there is more life to live (and more errors to make), you can put distance between yourself and regret.

5. If necessary, make corrections.
Similar to how forgiving oneself may offer a sense of relief, sometimes your regrets are about other people. It's appropriate to apologize and make amends wherever feasible. If, for example, you regret not seeing your family when you had the chance (i.e., before the pandemic), you might phone them and apologize for that.

In other instances, though, reaching out may not be appropriate or even possible. Regrets may lead us to believe that apologizing to our middle school ex is sensible. There's nothing wrong with that, but make sure you check in with yourself first. "Contacting the person 30 years later might not be acceptable," Dr. Allan explains. It could be okay to contact out if you believe your delayed apologies would be of genuine service to someone. It can be preferable to handle things independently if you're the only one who will feel better afterward.

6. Make a list of your regrets (then fact-check them).
It may sound contradictory, but writing about your regrets might be helpful if you find yourself thinking about them.

Writing down your negative ideas allows you to double-check them. Could it have affected your life if you had gone to an alternate school? You may add some skepticism and perspective to your narrative by writing it down.

Let's pretend that you write down your college regrets, fact-check them, and determine that your life may have turned out completely differently. Specificity, on the other hand, is on your side. If you wish you had been more confident in the past, you may work on that now. Alternatively, if you believe that a greater education would have prepared you for a new career path, it may be time to look into a few options for taking courses in the future. It's vital to remember that you're far more complicated than one regret, whether you recognize it or not. Dr. Roese clarifies, "It's not your entire life."

7. Try grief journaling.

Regret is a sort of sadness in certain aspects. Often, you're lamenting unfulfilled dreams for yourself or a future that may never come true. It's also conceivable that your regrets stem from losing a loved one. In certain instances, keeping a grieving notebook might help you work through your feelings. You can write down anything you're feeling in your journal. However, you can also write about other challenging events or faults you've encountered, as well as how you dealt with them. Instead of focusing on what you believe to be true about your regret (e.g., "I'll never be the same"), consider a list of future questions: What do I need from this moment? I can't alter what happened in the past, but how do I want to spend my time now and in the future? You may also free write and review your work later to observe how your attitude toward regret has evolved.

8. Look for those who have the same regrets as you.

Regret is a natural human emotion, and even though some people claim, "I don't spend my life with regrets," there's a chance they've experienced something similar. Instead of focusing on your problem, ask if any of your friends have experienced something similar or if you can locate tales and support groups dedicated to those who have had similar challenges. Dr. Roese adds that regrets are myopic; thus, talking to other people and listening to other people's experiences helps broaden your perspective beyond the present time.

9. If your ideas are affecting your mood, talk to someone. According to Dr. Roese, ruminating on regrets can increase symptoms of mental health concerns like depression, so if your regrets seem overwhelming, if they're causing depressed or anxious thoughts, or if you're starting to feel overwhelmed, get help from a mental health expert. Working with a therapist one-on-one can help you process your feelings.

How to let go of Denial

After a breakup, are you in denial? In a relationship where you're stuck in denial? Do you want to learn how to let go of your denial? Then you've arrived at the correct location. We'll figure out what it is, why we get into it, how to detect the indications, and how to get rid of it... so you can break free from terrible situations and go ahead.

So What Is Denial?

What exactly is denial? Isn't it a little ridiculous? Denial, as we all know, is the act of denying something.

"The state of refusing to accept the truth or existence of" or "the refusal to offer (something sought or wanted) to (someone)" is the definition. However, denial is more than a simple definition.

Denial is, at its core, a coping technique. By refusing to embrace the truth about what's going on in your life, you're attempting to shield yourself from the things that scare you or make you feel out of control.

You're terrified of what it will mean to confront it, so you're either giving yourself time to acclimate to a difficult circumstance or - even worse – attempting to avoid it entirely.

The problem is that it's akin to burying your head in the sand. At the moment, you may feel safe and comfortable. But it's simply a false sense of security that lasts a short time because you're ultimately hiding from reality.

It will not make the problem go away or change. In reality, taking charge of the situation is the only way to change it. When you live in denial, you typically make things worse.

We see this a lot in toxic relationships and after traumatic breakups. That is why you must be courageous. To confront what you don't want to face. Denial otherwise becomes a rejection to allow YOURSELF actual freedom.

Signs You're In Denial

You can be in denial about things that are occurring (or have occurred) to you, about things that are happening (or have happened) to others, and about things that are happening (or have happened) in general.

As an example, as previously said, a sour relationship is a scenario that affects both you and another person.

When you refuse to acknowledge a bad circumstance, you're most likely in denial. You know it shouldn't be this way, but you create exceptions, make explanations, try to rationalize it, or brush it off.

You might also try to avoid confronting the problem's reality by convincing yourself that it isn't true. Alternatively, you might be downplaying the issue's potential ramifications.

Denial can also manifest itself in the following ways:

- Avoid discussing the concerns.
- Making commitments you know you won't be able to keep or 'believing' promises you know won't be fulfilled.
- Trying to justify your (or someone else's) actions.
- Placing blame on others for an issue you created.
- Ignoring loved ones' counsel and worries.
- Taking a protective stance or fully shutting yourself off from others.
- Putting TOO MUCH EFFORT INTO FIXING SOMETHING to avoid acknowledging how horrible things are.
- Allowing, forgiving, and tolerating far more than you should.

You may be furious, anxious, annoyed, detached, or simply unhappy. Living in denial has a significant impact on your mental condition daily.

How To Let Go Of Denial

So, how do you go about it? What is the best way to let go of denial? The first step is to admit that you're in denial, which might be the most difficult aspect—recognizing but also acknowledging it.

Recognize You're In Denial

The good news is that if you have made it this far, there's a part of you that knows you're in denial about something.

Hopefully, the signals we discussed above have clarified this for you, and this post as a whole has clarified it for you - brought it to the surface, to your notice.

It's possible that it doesn't come as a full shock either. Maybe you've always known you've been in denial, but you've never labeled it as such or allowed yourself to go any farther.

Now that you've done so acknowledge it. Ensure you get what the issue is. Make quick work of things. Be honest with yourself.

Verbalize It To Make It Real

Once you've properly digested it in your mind, the following step is to verbalize it. It's smart to examine it with a companion or relative. It's time to get it off your chest. Someone can then hold you "accountable" in some way.

This is a crucial section. When you say it out loud, you share it with someone else, and it becomes true. You've come out of hiding. You must recognize it, accept it, and take action.

Otherwise, it's all too simple to retreat into your brain and push it away... which is precisely what denial wants us to do. So don't let that happen. TAKE ADVANTAGE OF THE MOMENT. SEIZE THIS POWER RIGHT NOW by reclaiming it.

To better understand your concerns and anxieties, talk to a friend or family member if you're in denial in a relationship and don't want to talk to your spouse about it just yet.

Remember that it doesn't necessarily have to be a horrible thing when you confront denial. It isn't necessarily anything to be afraid of. You typically avoid facing it because it brings about change - it forces you to step outside of your comfort zone, which may be frightening.

And, before you ask, what's so difficult about letting go of the denial you had about what your last relationship was truly like? Isn't it a positive thing that you can perceive and express? Yes, it is. But it's still difficult to accomplish since it contradicts your previous beliefs.

It's altering your perspective on the connection and what it all means. And seeing the world through rose-tinted glasses isn't always pleasant — it might make you feel as if you've wasted time or that the things you thought were real aren't. That brings me to my next point...

Understand What You're Afraid Of

To learn how to let go of denial, you must first comprehend why you were in denial in the first place.

- What are you afraid of? What's the big deal about that?
- What have you been attempting to avoid in terms of repercussions or outcomes?
- What is it about those things you are most afraid of?

Spin It Another Way

Whatever prompted your denial in the first place, whatever you were afraid of, I want you to consider this: Is there even a remote chance that the things you're afraid of will not occur?

Is there any way to keep your fears from becoming a reality? Make it less probable for them to happen?

What's the other side of this... what good might it do?

And how much is it costing you right now to be in denial? Consider how you're feeling, how you're feeling monetarily, or how you're evaluating things like time, which you'll never get back.

Stir Up That Emotion

All of the above questions will cause you to begin to THINK... which is fantastic. We moved from avoiding it to confronting it, and now we're delving even deeper. It will begin to modify your perspective and encourage your thoughts to search for answers.

To expand on this, come up with as many reasons as you can for why you need to let go of the denial and as many bad repercussions as you can for what will happen if you don't.

The simplest method to achieve this is to WRITE DOWN YOUR ANSWERS TO THE QUESTIONS ABOVE. Write down your replies and consider as many possibilities as you can from both sides. Activate that feeling. Then, when it's at its pinnacle, use it to your advantage.

Take Immediate Action

Do something at that moment that will force you to stop living in denial. The goal is to be in that condition when you're at your best. As a result, you won't be able to back out.

So, let's assume you're in denial about your relationship, and you've previously told someone you love and trust about it, but you didn't have the confidence to tell your partner because you were afraid of what would happen next.

You might take quick action by messaging your spouse and stating, "I'd like to chat to you about something later, please; it's crucial." You've committed to it if you say it. Then you can build on it and start putting stuff out there. "I know it's difficult to talk about, but I don't think this relationship is working anymore," you can remark. And I'm not saying this to start a fight or to force an end to it. I'm saying it because we need to discuss it right now. If we want to work on it and improve it, we need to talk about it."

This is where communication and understanding how to approach things properly come into play – but these are all skills that can be learned and practiced.

Regardless, you must make a living in denial, no longer an option if you wish to let go of it.

Let it Go

The most beautiful thing
we can learn, is how to let go;
of grudges, the past,
poisonous people.
It's a great measure
of courage.
Lessons Learned in Life

HOW TO LET GO OF CLUTTER IN YOUR SPIRITUAL LIFE.

Most of our houses have gathered a lot of things by the end of the year and might appear cluttered at times. We all need to do decluttering our houses from time to time, whether it's in the fall or the spring.

Our emotions and brains may accumulate dust and clutter like our physical spaces. We might become so engrossed in "things" that we lose sight of what matters — time with God.

Is it time to clear some space in your spiritual life?

Why Do I Need to Declutter My Spiritual Life

Our lives may be taken over by clutter in our houses. We're seeking stuff we want but can't find amid too many chaotic heaps.

Those crammed closets and overflowing "junk" drawers (I have two!) appear to be begging us to clean them out.

In our spiritual life, the same thing might happen. We can accumulate spiritual clutter to the point that the only areas left for God are the nooks and crevices between everything. How can someone fill you up when there's no room in your life for him?

Types of Spiritual Clutter

Having too much "spiritual baggage" can impede your relationship with your higher self.

Excessive social media, news, Netflix, or screen time can clog your thoughts.

Trying to juggle a hectic schedule might cause us to lose out on the greater plans for us. Are we spending quality time with our higher self as we engage in our favorite spiritual hustle and bustle, at church or in a group?

We might be drawn away from our higher connection if we become preoccupied with our desires and demands.

It's all too simple to shove our selfish behaviors into a garbage drawer. Resentments, bitterness, pride, and rage are all behaviors that stand in the way of our relationship with our higher self.

What emotional, spiritual junk do you keep in your spiritual closet? Fear, anxiety, worry, guilt, and shame may infiltrate your thoughts and suffocate the joy, peace, and happy spirit that your higher self-desires for you.

It's time to take action to improve your spiritual health once you've found your "messiest" spiritual closet(s).

Steps to Declutter your Spiritual Life

Look inwards

Ask your higher self to perform the cleansing as you begin the procedure. Request that he demonstrate what he wants you to let go of. He could astound you! What you see as unnecessary clutter might be where he has big intentions for you and vice versa.

Unpack Your Clutter

Like any other decluttering method, you must bring out all of the "stuff" and set it out. Decide which spiritual closet you wish to clean out and then sort through everything. Consider this: What activity or practice helps you grow spiritually?

What hinders you from hearing Jesus' voice and distracts you?

Is it for the glory of your higher self?

Bringing the eternal power honor should be our motivation in all we do – or don't do.

Take your time unpacking; don't rush it. Stop if you become overwhelmed. Start the next day again.

Release and Surrender

What activities do you need to preserve, and which ones do you need to let go of? Is it time to decline an invitation to join a club, study, or class? It is not unaware to say "no" to an opportunity! Release yourself if it isn't nourishing your soul or getting you closer to your soul.

Is there something from a former season of your life that you can let go of?

What are some of the bad feelings you'd like to give to the eternal spirit? Give him your pains, unpleasant memories, and losses.

Have you received a push or a call from your higher self in a certain area that you're considering? Do you have a desire to serve Him in some capacity, but you've tucked it away somewhere? Pull them out and lay them in His hands with care.

Organize the Good Stuff

Allow the eternal Spirit or your higher self ' to lead, reorient, and direct you during some quiet time with Him. He intends to provide you with all you require. Listen to your inner voice, as all the wisdom traditions of any faith remind us.

Decide what should be your top focus in life. Reintroduce them into your life with caution.

Rest in your higher Self Presence

You've done it! Congratulations! No schedule, study, or activity can provide us with what we most desire: rest in yourself.

PHYSICAL CLUTTER AND MENTAL CLUTTER

Mental clutter is anything that makes our thoughts feel like they're on overdrive. It's the ideas we have when awake, and while we all know that thinking is a necessary part of life, certain of our thoughts might make it difficult to focus.

This is how mental clutter might appear.

An overabundance of information I've already mentioned is, but in a nutshell, it's having too much information to comprehend, which causes mental exhaustion.

Expectations. This is when we want things or people around us to be a certain way, but they don't. It may be how you want your spouse to hang the dish towel or how you hope people would act better on Facebook comments.

Tasks that we're putting off. Making that phone call, folding these clothes, paying that charge. These things are always at the back of our minds.

Negative emotions. Stress, anxiety, worry, fear, embarrassment, wrath, and frustration are all negative emotions that annoy us.

We become frustrated, distracted, and unable to focus throughout the day if we do not learn to silence the chatter in our thoughts.

In a matter of seconds, we go from "What about that news from Florida?" to "I need to write that email!" to "That Instagram caption!" to "Where does Meghan Markle live?"

According to science, being psychologically overburdened has a bad impact on us and can contribute to burnout and failure to fulfill our tasks. A lack of mental space exacerbates anxiety and poor decision-making.

As a result of the overwhelm, we procrastinate by doing activities that make us feel better. You know how it feels when you don't want to think and instead watch TV till late at night.

Impact of Clutter on Mental Health

This physical, mental, and emotional clutter can make it difficult to think properly, leading to tension and exhaustion.

Clutter may make getting things done, finding what you need, and living in an ordered and effective manner difficult. We can feel anxious and worried if we spend time hunting for our keys or that one pair of jeans every day, allowing this negative daily energy to build up over time.

Sifting through physical clutter to find anything can take a significant amount of time, possibly detracting from other vital chores and self-care routines.

Excessive Clutter

When physical clutter gets overwhelming, it can threaten to entrap a person in problematic home surroundings, contributing to emotional anguish and emotions of displacement and loneliness.

Your house should be your refuge, a secure place where you can unwind. Still, when it's overrun by physical clutter, it may make you feel like it's your adversary rather than your sanctuary, severely impacting your overall well-being.

Clutter Can Impact Your Social Life

When our homes are cluttered, we may find it difficult to use the space for activities we like, such as yoga or crafting. We may also be ashamed to invite visitors over, significantly influencing our social lives, making us feel lonely and inadequate.

You probably have too much physical clutter in your life if you have problems tossing things away or feel overwhelmed by the amount of stuff you have in your house.

When Clutter Leads to Hoarding

Physical clutter may become an obsession—a need to acquire more material possessions to fill a gap. Sometimes we find ourselves surrounded by so many things that we can't bear to get rid of since it holds sentimental worth for us or may provide us with future happiness.

The unwillingness to get rid of items, regardless of their worth, is a symptom of hoarding disorder. Those who suffer from hoarding disorder find it challenging to manage their belongings.

The hoarding problem causes people to keep and store various stuff without any sort of organizing plan, to the point where their surroundings might become dangerous.

Individuals with hoarding disorder are more likely to preserve objects with sentimental significance or items they believe they may need in the future. Hoarding disorder may disrupt practically every area of a person's life, including personal relationships, career responsibilities, and social commitments.

Negative Consequences of Hoarding

Safety and health problems, such as fire dangers, tripping hazards, and health code violations, are possible repercussions of significant hoarding. Relationship difficulties, solitude, and the inability to do every day cooking and bathing can result from hoarding.

Hoarders may display the following characteristics:

- Inability to get rid of things.
- Severe anxiety while trying to get rid of things.
- Organizing possessions is difficult.
- Anxiety or shame regarding the size of one's personal belongings.
- Suspicion that other individuals are handling the stuff.
- Anxiety over running out of something or requiring it in the future.
- Functional impediments include a lack of living space, social isolation, family or marital strife, and financial problems.

Although not everyone who has clutter in their house will develop a hoarding condition, it is impossible to discuss the mental health repercussions of clutter without mentioning hoarding.

Mental Health Benefits of Decluttering (letting go of clutter)

Most people experience increased tension when they are in an untidy atmosphere. In one research, women who used positive language to describe their houses had lower levels of the stress hormone cortisol than women who used negative language.

Even still, the case for decluttering isn't straightforward. According to another study, while tidy surroundings are connected to healthier choices, chaotic environments foster innovation and new ideas. If you value creativity, you should permit yourself to be a little sloppy in certain aspects of your life.

Decluttering may boost productivity and enhance mental and physical health for most individuals. Better attention is one of the advantages of decluttering. It's tough to find what you're looking for when there's a lot of stuff around. It may also serve as a source of distraction. Getting rid of visual clutter might help you concentrate better on whatever activity you're working on.

Self-esteem is improved. As a result of a lack of organization, you may feel as if you're in charge of your life. Improving your living area might help you regain confidence and pride in yourself.

It improved interpersonal interactions. When one individual can't regulate clutter, it might conflict with family or housemates. You may also feel more at ease welcoming guests into your house if it is clean.

Asthma and allergy symptoms are reduced. Even if it appears cluttered, your house is clean. However, it is tough to clean around a lot of clutter. Asthma and allergies can be made worse by pests, mold, and mildew accumulated in cluttered spaces.

It improved well-being and lifestyle. In a clean kitchen, it's simpler to cook healthful meals. In addition, most individuals sleep better in a clean room with a clean bed.

You'll decrease your stress and anxiety levels.
It's no secret that clutter makes us feel anxious. The more "stuff" we have in front of us, the more reminders we have of all we need to accomplish.

Seeing enormous stacks of dishes, unfolded clothing, or unreviewed documents may increase your worry and tension. Worse, the clutter-anxiety cycle feeds off of itself and feels unavoidable. Clearing your space will help you to cleanse your mind.

You'll feel physically healthier.
When you have a lot of clutter, you're inviting a lot of dust into your home. Asthma and other respiratory illnesses may be worse or worsened due to this. Even if you don't have asthma, the detrimental respiratory consequences of dust stacking up and contaminating your air quality might be felt. You'll notice a difference in your breathing and bodily well-being once you've cleaned up your surroundings.

Your productivity will improve.
Organize your workspace and keep it as simple as possible. Clutter raises the chances of being distracted. Whether it's an electronic item or a mountain of work piling up on your

desk, everything has to be put in its rightful place. When your workspace is clean and tidy, you'll find it much simpler to work efficiently.

Learning to reduce things to their bare essence.
You'll need to develop some great organizational skills once you start removing the clutter from your life. Begin by re-evaluating your home's essentials and getting rid of the things you should've gotten rid of a long time ago. When you want to see substantial changes in your attitude, the best place to start is by decluttering your house. It's time to let go of items that have no purpose, don't offer you any joy, or that you've forgotten about.

Adopt a minimalistic mindset to live a cleaner and more orderly life. Some individuals cling to the concept of having, spending, and wanting less. Begin by getting rid of all of the items you no longer require. This includes outdated magazines, clothes you don't wear anymore, and other products you don't use.

You'll have to start making greater adjustments and removing more from your life, which might be frightening. Don't be put off by the terrible connotations of this chopping down. You don't have to live with less in your life; instead, you've chosen to be free of all your belongings.

You'll want to deliberate about what you consider your basics. Don't scrimp on the essential elements of your house after you've decided on them. Living with less allows you to invest in higher-quality products that will last longer. Consider the most basic goods in your home:

- The kitchen needs for eating.
- The bathroom necessities for remaining clean.
- The bedroom necessities for obtaining the rest you require.

Having worked out what you need, it's possible to start afresh from scratch. More sunshine will enter your house, less dust will accumulate, and you will have a higher chance of raising your productivity and improving your mood.

How to let go of mental clutter

To have a cluttered mind is worse than having a jam-packed home or office. A crowded mind is distracted and restless. It attempts to go in many different ways at once, and as a result, it accomplishes very little.

Worrying about the future, obsessing about the past, having a mental to-do list, complaining, and so on are all examples of mental clutter. There are, fortunately, ideas and procedures you may employ to clear some mental space.

Here are some ideas for clearing your mind:

Declutter Your Physical Environment.

Mental clutter is caused by physical clutter. To begin with, clutter overloads the mind with stimuli, forcing the brain to work overtime. Second, physical clutter sends a message to the brain that there's always something else to do, which is cognitively draining. You'll find that decluttering your physical area also declutters your thinking.

Set Priorities

"The difficulty with not having a goal is that you might spend your life running up and down the field and never score," wrote famous American poet Bill Copeland.

Prioritizing is an excellent approach to taking control of your life. The first stage is identifying the most important things to you, your life goals, and your long-term objectives. List your top priorities and check to see that your behaviors and decisions are by them. The next stage is to make an action plan to achieve your objectives and figure out how you'll split your time to focus on each item on your list. It's essential to remember that your priorities may shift as you get older, and that's fine as long as you check in with yourself regularly to make sure they're still serving you well.

Keep A Journal

Journaling is a terrific technique to calm your mind. According to a study published in the Journal of Experimental Psychology, in general, expressive writing minimizes intrusive thoughts about bad occurrences and enhances the working memory. Researchers anticipate that these gains will free up our cognitive resources for other mental processes, such as better stress management. A study conducted by the University of Rochester Medical Center found that keeping a daily journal helped those with anxiety and depression by allowing them to get their feelings out into the open. You don't need to be a prolific writer to start a journal. Bullet journaling is one of the easiest strategies to try out for beginners.

Learn To Let Go

"Take a deep breath, embrace who you are now, and keep going." "If you want to soar, you must give up what weighs you down," writes Roy T. Bennett in his book The Light in the Heart. It's critical to let go of all the bad feelings and ideas weighing you down. Reduce stress, enhance self-esteem, and free up brain space by removing unneeded thoughts, anxieties, and concerns. Regularly monitor your thoughts and strive to replace negative ones with good ones.

Multitasking should be avoided.

It appears to be counter-productive. But believe me when I say that preparing your office presentation while updating your Instagram and searching for a secret Santa gift for your roommate on the internet isn't useful. While there's nothing wrong with occasional multitasking, doing so regularly reduces your attention span, raises stress, and adds to the clutter by making it tough for your brain to filter out unnecessary data. Stanford University researchers found that multitasking significantly reduces productivity and may impede cognitive control. The idea is to focus on one thing at a time as much as possible. Make a list of everything you want to get done that day. Keep your to-do list short and to the point. Start with the essential item on the list and work your way down the list, one task at a time.

Limit the amount of data that comes in.

The brain may get clogged with too much information. This includes the information you get each day from newspapers, blogs, and magazines, as well as information you get from watching TV, engaging in social media, and surfing the web on your smartphone.

Limit the quantity of information that enters your life—and free up mental space in the process—by performing the following:

Set a time limit for how much time you'll spend on social networking sites or surfing the internet.

Don't subscribe to any blogs or magazines that don't make you happy or improve your quality of life.

Make sure the perspectives you listen to are from well-known people and have relevant qualifications.

Decide what information is important to you and ignore the rest.

Make a decision.

What happens if your inbox is overflowing with documents and you can't decide what to do with each one? Your inbox will soon be flooded with messages, bills, and queries from potential clients, among other things. One way to declutter your inbox is to decide what to do with each piece of paper.

Your brain is the same. The more time you put off making a decision, the more options you have to choose from. Determination is the key.

Follow Benjamin Franklin's advice and make a pros-and-cons list for basic decisions. Apply a complete technique, such as the WRAP Method advised by the Heath brothers in their book "Decisive: How to Make Better Choices in Life and Work," when you need to make more critical and difficult decisions.

Put all of your routine decisions on autopilot.

Small, repetitive chores may take up a lot of mental real estate. This can involve a variety of things, such as:

Deciding what to eat for breakfast each morning, what to dress each day, what to eat for lunch, and so on.

By placing these typical processes on auto-pilot, you can free up space for other things in your brain. For example, "The Big Bang Theory," a popular TV comedy in which the four main characters are very bright physicists, is a good example. Sheldon Cooper, for example, is a big fan of routines and has one for just about everything.

Some instances are as follows:
For each day of the week, he wears a different pair of underpants and a different t-shirt.

Sheldon eats the same thing for breakfast and dinner every day (for example, he eats with his friends every Tuesday night at The Cheesecake Factory).

Every Saturday at 8:15 p.m., Sheldon does the laundry, just one of his established many routines.

Although Sheldon oversteps the mark, the point is well made. It's time to put as many tiny, ordinary jobs out of your mind as possible.

Breathe

Take a deep breath in and out. Pause. Slowly exhale. Repeat. How does it make you feel? Isn't it fantastic? Deep breathing is a simple yet powerful method for clearing your thoughts, inducing calmness, and quickly elevating your mood. It helps your body relax by lowering your heart rate and blood pressure and stimulating the parasympathetic nervous system. Breathing exercises ease the tension and improve focus and build your immune system.

Organize Your Workspace.

Did you know that people who work in a cluttered environment are less productive and irritated than those who work at a well-organized desk? So now you know! So don't put off decluttering your desk till tomorrow; do it today. Start by getting rid of any non-essential objects and putting everything in its correct location. Cleaning up your work desk every day before going home is the greatest way to keep things orderly without feeling overwhelmed or fatigued.

Share Your Thoughts

Talking to a loved one about how you're feeling is a terrific method to get your feelings out. Sharing your opinions with others may also help you see things in a new light, allowing you to think more clearly and make better judgments.

Take Some Time To Relax: Finally, but certainly not least, take a break! Your brain needs to relax and recharge in order to function properly. So put down your phones and laptops and do something that brings you joy. It doesn›t matter if it›s a long snooze or a stroll around the park.

Put your ideas on paper.

Taking all those thoughts and writing them down is one of the finest strategies to clear your mind. Putting them down on paper helps you let go of the obligation of remembering them and cleaning your thoughts in the process.

Suppose you're the type of person continuously coming up with new ideas (which is fantastic!). In that case, you might consider finding a means to store them rather than holding them all in your mind, which could rapidly become overwhelming. To clear your mind, consider downloading an app or bringing a tiny notebook with you to jot down your new thoughts. The idea is to choose one storage location and keep to it, so you know where to look for them.

Negativity must be confronted.

Negativity can be crippling and take up a lot of mental space. Sadness and disappointment are natural feelings, but poisonous self-talk increases your misfortune and distorts your perspective of reality.

Start by becoming aware of how you talk to yourself. What are you saying to yourself? Keep an eye out for warning signs, such as victimizing attitudes ("poor me" thinking). It's time to shift your thinking if the ideas in your head or the words on your paper after your writing practice are poisonous self-talk.

You need to start challenging yourself if you want to improve your way of thinking. Is the thought correct, or has it been skewed? Your mind will begin to replace negative ideas with positive ones as you show yourself that your negative self-talk is erroneous. As a result, your mind will transition from feeling heavy, crowded, and chaotic (negativity) to feeling lighter and free (positivity).

One aspect of pushing oneself is to begin accumulating more pleasant experiences. By doing anything to improve your or someone else's life a little better, you may practice appreciation and compassion. Do something to help yourself or someone else when you notice yourself thinking badly. The next time you have negative self-talk, you'll be able to see that your brain isn't always correct.

Find time for you

Don't undervalue the significance of taking care of yourself and making time for yourself. It's now your turn to do whatever you want, from reading a book to practicing karate. I'm sure you spend a lot of your time doing things for other people, so set aside some time each day to do something just for you.

Make specific goals for yourself.

Make a list of goals to help you find direction and concentration in your life. It's OK to fly by the seat of your trousers or to be sheltered by the powerful winds of life now and then. However, if you want things to happen in your life and build a wonderful life for yourself and your family, you'll probably benefit from setting a few objectives and making a strategy to attain them. "A goal without a strategy is merely a dream," said Antoine de Saint-Exupéry.

Have healthy habits

Develop everyday practices that are both physically and emotionally beneficial. Check your eating habits, choose nutritious foods and diets, set aside time for self-improvement and learning new skills, cultivate mutually supportive relationships, don't go to bed too late, and wonder why you press the snooze button in the morning! Look at these healthy behaviors to incorporate into your everyday routine for additional ideas.

Work-life balance is important.

Strive to discover ways to balance work and home life as much as possible by limiting the number of hours you spend working. Time for your family, your interests, and time for you. They're all crucial. Keep an eye out for signals that your work-life balance is off, and take action before it takes you down.

Practice meditation

Meditation requires practice, and I must admit that I am not very good at it! Persistence, though, pays off, and I've discovered that guided meditations available on the internet are quite helpful in getting me in the correct frame of mind. If you want to learn more, go visit Headspace.com or a meditation class. One of the best ones is OHIA meditation, Berlin.

Don't cram too much into your schedule.

Keep an eye on your calendar, and if it becomes too hectic and you don't have time to breathe, don't be afraid to cancel or postpone events. Create free time to relieve stress, leave yourself some wiggle room for emergencies, do things on the spur of the moment, run late for appointments, and simply enjoy doing whatever you want once in a while.

Reduce the number of decisions you make daily.

You should limit your everyday decisions if you wish to decrease mental overwhelm.

Many of the choices we make are so insignificant that they don't warrant your attention or mental energy.

Making a weekly food plan and arranging your clothing for the following day before going to bed is the simplest way to get started.

By making these tiny modifications in the morning before starting your day, you may save a lot of time and mental energy.

In addition, I strongly advise you to organize your weeks and days ahead of time. This will assist you in being more organized and reducing the number of unforeseen circumstances and deadlines.

Less growing, more dreaming.

We sometimes forget to pause because we are so accustomed to the hustling culture.

Learning, improving, and working toward your objectives are all vital, but you need breaks to perform at your best in the long term.

Allow yourself some time to fantasize instead of continually assaulting your head with fresh must-dos and facts.

You don't have to keep learning and growing all the time. You may sometimes just enjoy the moment and let your thoughts wander.

Stop attempting to make the most of every minute. Take a stroll, listen to music instead of podcasts or audiobooks, read more nonfiction books, and give your mind a chance to rest.

How to declutter(let go) your physical clutter.

Excessive clutter is a common symptom and source of stress, and it may influence every aspect of your life, from the amount of time it takes you to complete tasks to your money and general enjoyment of life. Clutter may cause you to become distracted, weigh you down, and generally bring turmoil into your life.

If you don't know where or how to begin, clearing the clutter might appear to be an impossible undertaking. You'll enjoy the benefits of beautiful living environments, decreased stress, and a more organized and productive existence by dedicating a little time to getting rid of the clutter in your life and keeping things generally clutter-free.

Being organized may seem like an overwhelming undertaking at first, but it does not have to be. Small measures taken together will provide large results that will be simpler to maintain in the long run.

Having a lot of possessions was once considered a sign of wealth. The wealthiest households have the largest residences and lavishly decorated rooms. Women used to wear obscene amounts of jewelry, which made their affluence clear at first glance.

Even a large belly was a sign of affluence in ancient Rome since it signified you could afford to eat a lot, which wasn't the case for the majority of the populace.

Nonetheless, the last several decades have altered how we think and live.

Most individuals know that health equals wealth and strive to keep their stomachs small rather than large.

Similarly, more individuals opt for a minimalist lifestyle in Western nations, reducing clutter, and designing their houses and lifestyles in basic ways.

In light of our admittance to the web and the gigantic volume of advertisements we are presented to, we are now confronting a significant data flood.

That's why so many individuals reduce their possessions and simplify their lives.

According to Jim Kwik, we now consume as much data in a single day as the average person in the 1400s did in their lifetime.

This exemplifies why we frequently feel overwhelmed and fatigued even though we don't do much.

The fact is that most of the items you own and retain are unnecessary.

You don't need a phone full of screenshots or a closet full of clothes and sneakers.

Having many possessions necessitates a greater level of organization and cleanliness. This is both time-consuming and draining on the mind.

And, as busy as we all are, we want to maintain our minds clear and fresh rather than overwhelmed.

Decluttering is all about reducing the amount of turmoil in your life. You'll have more time and energy to deal with unforeseen events if you do so. You'll also truly be able to experience your favorite pastimes.

While some individuals can effortlessly disregard clutter and distractions, I find it difficult to work at my best when I lack mental and physical clarity.

Decluttering regularly allows me to be more organized in all aspects of my life while also reducing anxiety and overwhelm.

Physical declutter

Three forms of clutter frequently surround us: Clutter in the physical, digital, and psychic realms.

Even though they all have a detrimental influence on our lives, I recommend beginning with physical decluttering because it may assist the other two areas.

"In the absence of an idea of what is necessary or beautiful, you should not keep anything in your home at all."

— William Morris.

Simply said, physical decluttering entails tossing stuff out, cleaning, and tidying up.

It's all about making extra room so your belongings don't get in the way.

The majority of individuals could simply get rid of at least half of the goods in their homes: Clothes, dishes, old paperwork, and so forth...

However, we are frequently emotionally linked to our possessions, making decluttering a time-consuming and difficult task.

Despite my attachment to my tangible stuff, here's how I declutter:

Sort out seasonal and occasional things

You may have a lot of important stuff that you don't use daily.

This might include sporting equipment (e.g., skiing) or clothing for special events.

Even though they take up room, you can't get rid of them since you know you'll need them in the future, and you don't want to have to buy them all over again.

That is why it is critical to organize these items and recognize that you will need them on occasion. This also makes it easy to hide them in your basement, so they aren't in your way all of the time.

The emotional tie

We sometimes maintain things because we have an emotional attachment to them. We don't need or use most of these items, but we have difficulty putting them away since they remind us of specific events or individuals.

Decluttering shouldn't be painful in general. You don't want to make yourself toss memories away.

Instead, you want to loosen your emotional attachment to material possessions so you may devote more attention to new experiences.

If you must preserve specific objects because of an emotional attachment, make sure to store them appropriately so you can harness their good energy rather than letting them collect dust in a corner.

The six-month rule

Tossing things that we think we'll need in the future may be challenging for some.

For example, you could lose weight in a few months and be able to wear your snug pants again.

If you're on the fence about keeping something, ask yourself if you've used it in the last six months.

If you don't use it now, you're unlikely to use it in the following six months.

Another question that may help you weed out unnecessary products is: Would I buy this if I were shopping right now?

Marie Kondo, an organization guru, recommends getting rid of anything that doesn't bring you joy.

According to her, we should only own and retain objects that make us truly happy or are required.

If you wouldn't buy a product or item of apparel again, you can usually get rid of it without too much difficulty.

Finally, consider whether the object you want to keep symbolizes the person you want to be.

It makes sense to possess clothes that make you feel more confident if you want to be more confident. The same goes for whatever else you own and use - put your possessions to the test by asking yourself if your best self would utilize them.

If, despite answering those questions, you still find it challenging to let go of specific objects, put them in a box, name them with the current date, and keep it for a few months.

You can take and utilize everything you've put in the box if you need it.

You can give or trash away whatever you don't need after a maximum of six months. This simple guideline ensures that you will not require those items in the future.

Minimizing storage space

We tend to keep more stuff when we have more room.

I enjoy purchasing new storage boxes to help me arrange my shelves and cabinets, but I try to limit my purchases to avoid creating extra room for clutter.

Most people are uncomfortable with empty shelves, although it just allows us to have greater mental space.

If you don't like the empty area, you may fill it with tiny decorative things that make your house more enjoyable.

Use labels and elastic bands

Nothing is more aggravating than scouring hundreds of shelves for an item you haven't used in a long time because you have no idea where to search.

And if there's anything more aggravating, it's dangling cables.

That's why I keep all of my miscellaneous items in little bins, mark them with sticky notes, and manage long cords with elastic bands.

Using vertical space

It's frequently feasible to make greater use of vertical space, but we seldom consider it since we're used to horizontal storage.

You may stack items to save space and appear more ordered when you store vertically.

This is especially effective with books or kitchen cabinets. You'll be able to make the most of your space while still keeping your countertop clean.

Apply Mise en Place

The French expression "mise in place" approximately translates to "everything in its place."

It's usually used in cooking to indicate that you've measured, sliced, peeled, and prepared all of your components before getting started.

However, mise en place may be applied to other aspects of your life, including your mental condition.

One approach to using mise en place is to make sure your work area is correctly set up before you begin working.

Restore order and cleanliness to the workspace once you've completed your task (or cooking).

You can use mise en place for anything else in your life in addition to the kitchen or at work.

It will be easier to immediately put items back where they belong when you aren't using them if you make sure they belong in a certain spot.

Designating a location for specific goods can make you feel more relaxed and assured because you won't have to look for them frantically.

Is there anything you need to ask yourself before purchasing any kind?

Decluttering only lasts if two guidelines are consistently followed:

Get rid of whatever you don't need.

Don't spend money on items you don't need.

If you embark on a weekly buying spree, even frequent decluttering won't help.

When I'm preparing to acquire something new, I follow these three steps:

Consider if you require or desire something.

This inquiry aims to limit the number of purchases that aren't helpful or wanted, not to stop buying items you want.

We frequently purchase items only because they are on sale or because we believe we will require them in the future.

These are poor decisions most of the time, and it is preferable to purchase items that you truly desire or require.

Would you purchase it if the price was doubled?

If you answered no, you probably don't require or desire it as much as you believed.

If none of these questions help you decide whether or not to buy anything, establish a time limit for yourself and make your decision after a few days.

Take a photo of a shirt you want to buy, leave it in the store, and only buy it if you can't stop thinking about it.

You know you don't need to buy anything if you forget about it after 48 hours.

How to Declutter Your Work Area

We're all surrounded by clutter, and now since many of us work from home, it's all day, every day.

Physical, emotional, and digital clutter, in my opinion, have taken over many of our lives. Those of you who habitually check your phones first thing in the morning are likely to find an overflowing inbox and messages. And once you're out of bed, you can find yourself strolling past "clutter traps," which include anything from the bathroom to the kitchen to your home office and laptop computer. I haven't even mentioned the possibility of a crowded to-do list in front of you.

As a professional organizer, I feel that decluttering is critical for today's business professionals, especially regarding our mental health. Even though I'm not a doctor, I've spent the last ten years researching this topic to encourage my clients and myself to declutter our lives in every way possible. According to The New York Times, Clunkiness can cause stress and harm your mental health. There's a link between clutter and procrastination as well.

I know how much serenity and joy I get from living in a clutter-free environment, both physically and psychologically. I'd also like you to consider your workstation and how it makes you feel. Do your surroundings make you feel overwhelmed, worried, or defeated?

The more crowded and less productive your working environment grows in many offices, the busier you are. Every team needs a method to keep things neat and organized to retain efficiency. This may appear to be a simple activity, but when we spend so much time in our workplaces, it's easy to grow acclimated to and even immune to the clutter. This frequently results in unforeseen organizational issues. The ability of a team to manage more challenging activities like distribution or QA workflows, such as keeping a workspace free of clutter and confusion, may sometimes be gauged by how well they can accomplish something as seemingly easy as this.

Tips for decluttering your office space work area and, consequently, becoming more productive.

Only keep the things you need

Rather than making individual judgments about what to keep and discard, it is sometimes preferable to get rid of everything and then gradually bring items back as needed. Consider it your computer's desktop. More shortcuts appear on the desktop backdrop when you add more programs. It's only after you've removed all of the shortcuts that you realize how little you used them.

The same approach applies to your office, whether at home or in a different location. It's typical to find objects in a work area that haven't been touched in months, but that doesn't mean they have to stay. Allowing them to take up valuable space while providing nothing to your productivity is a bad idea. You can more efficiently and objectively retain only the necessary by getting rid of everything and then bringing items back in as needed. Although this strategy may appear excessive, it is a fantastic way to rapidly identify which objects do not serve a function or obstruct your productivity (though we won't criticize you if you save a few items for sentimental reasons).

Practically organize your workspace.

Following the start from scratch technique to decrease clutter, the next step is to arrange the remaining objects in your workspace in order of how frequently you use them. You may use your fountain pen every day, but you're much more than likely to review your Human Resources manual every six months.

To optimize your efficiency, keep your most often used products (such as chargers and notebooks) in the top desk drawers, where they'll be easier to find. Keeping pens and pencils in a nearby cup is preferable to keeping additional supplies (such as headphones and staples). Arrange the remainder of the workplace in the same way, with your least-used stuff at the far end. This simple strategy will boost your productivity by ensuring that your most often used items are always near at hand while your other personal belongings are tucked away and off your desk.

Sort by "keep," "recycle/trash," and "belongs elsewhere."

There's a reason why leaders of all kinds use the rule of threes: it works. Create three boxes or bags: retain, recycle, or dispose, and place someplace else if you want to organize your supplies and possessions quickly. You should be able to put everything in its proper location. Even emotional people who like to cling to particular stuff might find new homes for their belongings while reducing clutter in the workplace. Consider which items may be recycled (papers and plastics) and discarded (empty bottles, flyers, and leaflets).

Get a handle on your cords.

The number of wires appears to expand exponentially in every workplace, from phone and laptop chargers to HDMI cords and headphone dongles. It might be a never-ending effort to keep those cords under control, whether they are on top of or below your desk. Some individuals opt to disregard this problem, but if a problem arises with any of your equipment, your lack of organization might create significant delays in finding and addressing the issue.

Investing in a Dymo Labeling system and labeling each cable as you install it in your business is a fantastic solution to this problem. The next step is to purchase a Cablox system, which will let you swiftly and efficiently organize your wires and, perhaps more significantly, ensure that they remain nice and tidy moving forward. You may also make labels and organize boxes out of film canisters, paper holders, shoeboxes, and other household things if you want to be creative and save money.

Take a photograph (you might be shocked)

Have you ever gone to other people's desks and spotted clutter that your coworker is blissfully ignorant of? The same is probably true in your workplace. Your guests will have a different perspective on your office and will be more aware of the clutter that you may not be aware of.

Taking a snapshot of your workplace from the entrance is a wonderful method to put this summary to the test. This will allow you to observe your working environment through the eyes of your visitors, and the results will astound you. If you're having problems spotting clutter, try photographing it from multiple perspectives. Photographs offer a unique viewpoint, and possible issues may appear in the image, allowing you to identify the parts that need to be cleaned up immediately.

Make a digital copy of your notes and papers.

Documents, business cards, sticky notes, meeting notes, and other paper-based clutter are likely to make up the majority of your clutter. Rather than keeping them on hand if you need them someday, digitize your papers by making electronic copies of them, either by scanning or typing them out.

Several apps on your smartphone allow you to scan and store documents fast and easily. Take images of important papers you can't afford to lose, then toss or recycle the paper copies. You may also use Evernote, Google Docs, Google Keep (a note), and the notes applications for iOS and Android phones as note-taking tools. Not only can you digitize notes using these applications, but you can also synchronize them across numerous devices via the cloud. If you have a stack of business cards on your desk, take images of them or add them to your contacts list before discarding them. One advantage of digitizing your documents is that you can quickly and easily look through them.

Get in the Zone

You can categorize and prioritize work if you organize your job activities based on zones on your desk. This can also help you psychologically shift as you physically move when you alter directions in your workflow throughout the day. Consider the following to get an idea of how you may divide your workspace into zones:

- A zone for research
- A zone for writing
- A zone to hold meetings
- A zone to answer the email

Get Away for Lunch

It's great that you packed your lunch and brought it to work, but you don't have to eat it all. Declutter your workstation of unneeded plates, utensils, storage containers, and food to become a better employee. Instead, take your lunch outdoors and enjoy it at a patio table with other coworkers. Eat at the break table at the office. Go somewhere else if you don't want to have your lunch at your desk.

What occurs when you take a break is a miracle worker for the exhausted employee. Employees who take a break from their workstations during the day, according to research, return with fresh enthusiasm and imagination for the tasks at hand. Everyone can take at least 20 minutes away from their workstation to have lunch if they arrange their day effectively. You'll clear your desk of food strewn about the office, and you'll refresh your mind for the hectic day ahead.

Toss and Delete

Getting rid of unnecessary paper and email is one of the most effective strategies to tidy and organize your workstation. Both paper copies and stuff you don't need stacking up on your desk, as well as digital files taking up space on your computer or in your email inbox, should be discarded. By approaching each file or document with a sense of urgency to get rid of it if you don't need it, you'll create a liberating environment that will not only make you feel freer and empowered but will also help you become more organized. There will be less to sift through (i.e., less time spent researching and searching) and more time on the project you need to do or the deadline you have to fulfill.

Sort through your digital photographs.

You may despise the idea, but in my opinion, it is pointless to save fresh images if your old photos are crowded, especially if your business relies on this sort of information.

What is the purpose of having images if you can't find the ones you want to share with your audience? To begin, my best advice is to buy an app that can assist you in deleting duplicates and unclear photographs.

Maintain control over your inbox.

Unsubscribe from emails daily. Make folders and get to know your email inbox and tabs for organizing. Most importantly, I advocate just checking your email twice a day and informing your clients and a team of the times you'll be reading messages so that an expectation can be established.

Finally, when you've completed these four simple steps, give your workstation a thorough professional cleaning. To clean dirt and spills:

1. Use disinfectant wipes.
2. Use a keyboard air gun to clean your keyboard and a professional screen cleaner and cloth to clean your computer monitor.
3. Vacuum your computer chair, dust it, and empty the trash bin.

Final cleaning is the final phase in the procedure, and it will help you feel more refreshed and ready to begin your workday!

Benefits of decluttering your workspace

An orderly office is more than a pleasant environment; it may also have psychological benefits. To put it another way, understanding how to organize your desk office or cubicle at work can lead to positive outcomes.

1. Improved impressions

If your manager notices clutter at your workplace regularly, they may have a negative impression of you. Your bosses or supervisors may believe you are uninterested in the job. If you're a salesperson, your sales manager may be concerned about the image your desk will make on customers, clients, or businesses with whom they're attempting to establish ties. When those in positions of authority at a company are pleased with your presence, you will be more driven.

2. Improved comfortability

You've probably tried to put an essential file on your desk before but couldn't find a place for it in your busy workspace. You may begin to feel hemmed in at your workstation. Keeping your desk clean might help you feel more at ease at work. Greater productivity can be achieved by creating more open space and a more pleasant workplace. Consider how difficult it is to perform a task when physically ill, and then apply that to this circumstance.

3. Boosted confidence

A crowded desk indicates that you have misplaced something at some time. Maybe your boss comes by to ask for a crucial document. Even if you could recover the file, you probably didn't make a good impression on your boss scrambling around to find it. You might feel more confident in your job when you can quickly create essential resources and don't have to move about your desk seeking them. Knowing that you're making a better impression on your bosses might help you feel even more confident.

4. Improved immunity

If you haven't had your desk professionally cleaned in a while, you could have germs on the surface from the ill coworker who dropped by. You might want to blame other individuals if you're continually recognizing that you're not feeling well. However, your workstation may be weakening your immune system. Workers in big cities like Detroit or Baltimore may already have weakened immune systems than those in the suburbs. There's no use in adding to the flames. Cleaning up the clutter and wiping down your desk with disinfectant might help reduce your risk of contracting an infection.

5. Accomplishment

You may feel as though you aren't adding anything to the environment or that you have ceased accomplishing milestones at work when things are moving slowly. While the ultimate objective is to be happy in your job, you may also celebrate tiny victories along the road. You may feel good about crossing something off your to-do list when you take the time to tidy your desk. Instead of looking at another assignment that hasn't been finished, you might feel proud of yourself for achieving a minor victory.

6. Dealing with procrastination

You could be a procrastinator, which explains why you're putting off organizing your crowded desk. When you notice work that looks too difficult to do, you tend to put it off. Unless your office requires you to clean and tidy your desk, you may never get around to it. It is, nonetheless, essential to understand how to prevent procrastinating. Procrastination has certain advantages, particularly for people who work best under pressure, but it can also result in you not getting anything done.

7. Building time management skills

Clearing your clutter may appear to be a big undertaking that will consume a significant portion of your workday. Resolving the matter may take some time, depending on how terrible it is. That isn't to say you have to do the assignment in one session or even one day. Make a plan instead of attempting to accomplish so. You might set aside a specific amount of time each day to concentrate on decluttering. This technique will assist you in developing better time management abilities, which you can subsequently use for your whole job.

How to let go of clutter in Your Home

Outside of work, we spend most of our time at home. It's no surprise, however, that a cluttered home may contribute to everyday stress.

Everyone has some clutter around the house – and most of us have a lot of it. However, many individuals feel anxious and as if their lives are out of control when surrounded by more things than they can handle.

Decluttering your house and cleaning up the debris is a great way to look after yourself. According to a Budget Dumpster poll, 75% of Americans had done a decluttering activity in the previous year.

Clutter is defined as everything you maintain that adds no value to your life. Making space in your house for the things that matter is the goal of decluttering.

When does clutter become an issue?

Many people find clutter to be a drain on their energy, as well as a waste of time spent searching for stuff they can't locate. Anxiety was reported by 48.5 percent of the participants who participated in our survey about having clutter in their homes. According to a survey, 42.5 percent of people asked claimed clutter made them feel uneasy. Disillusionment or obesity can result when a person's consumption extends beyond "things." Further health risks may emerge if mold and dust are present in more extreme hoarding circumstances. It's possible that a messy house could also be a fire hazard.

REASONS TO DECLUTTER YOUR HOME

Here are ten reasons to tidy your house and replace clutter with space. Take a look and see if any of them strike a chord with you.

1. Less stress

Our exterior settings (homes, businesses, and neighborhoods) impact our inner environments (our bodies and brains). Clutter has been demonstrated in scientific research to impact our capacity to focus and concentrate, and it has also been found to increase our stress levels.

2. More space

Getting rid of unnecessary clutter may seem self-evident, but it frees up physical space. You only maintain what you require, love, cherish, and provide worth to your life.

3. More peace

As a result of the visible and mental clutter that comes with too much clutter, your home will be calmer and more peaceful.

4. Easier to find things

Reduced clutter makes it easier to locate lost objects (and thus less likely that you'll lose anything). Even if you're not the most organized person, you'll be able to find what you're looking for faster because there is less clutter to go through. You will almost probably need to reorganize your possessions to declutter and determine what to keep and what to get rid of. Set up file systems, storage, or other places to hold things, so you'll know where they are at all times as part of this procedure.

5. Increases productivity and efficiency

Continuing from the previous point, you'll be more productive and efficient since you won't have to waste time looking for stuff!

6. Easier to look after

It is SO much simpler to care for and maintain a decluttered house. It's easier to tidy up, clear things away, clean, and stay on top of things when there's less junk around getting in the way. You'll have more time (and energy) to accomplish other things if you spend less time cleaning and caring for your house. If you establish some easy routines for your housework and regular duties, you can make caring for your home even faster and easier.

7. Ready for visitors

It's simpler to maintain your home appearing nice, tidy, and ready for visitors (pretty much) at all times if it's easy to care for and has less clutter. Yes, you'll probably need to rush about picking up a few things, but nothing that will take more than a few minutes or that your visitors would notice!

8. You'll spend less

When you become used to living with less clutter and learning to be more purposeful and aware about what you let into your house, you'll likely spend less money on things you don't truly need or desire. Instead of going shopping, you'll start to look for other methods to make yourself happy. It will also benefit your money account!

9. Encourages gratitude

Being appreciative of what you have and concentrating on what matters to you and your family is crucial, but it's easy to forget in today's consumerist culture. When we're accustomed to having a lot of things, it's easy to overlook what we already have. The same is true for adults and children who have so many toys that they don't know where to begin!

10. Less debt.

Spending less time shopping for material stuff and adding to the clutter means your wallet and bank accounts stay fuller, your credit card balances stay lower, and your house stays free of expensive items you don't need.

11. More financial freedom.

The majority of American families live paycheck to paycheck (59 percent according to a recent survey done by Charles Schwab back in May 2019.) Almost half of those polled have credit card debt. When you combine decluttering with minimalism, you'll be able to save money to protect yourself for an emergency.

12. More time and energy for other things
The objective isn't to have a clutter-free house. Although having an uncluttered, orderly, family-friendly, and welcome house (i.e., a decluttered home) is nice, the true magic is in what this decluttered home will provide you. You'll have more time, space, energy, freedom, and money. Consider what all of this could imply for you and your family. It's all about identifying your priorities and striking a balance between taking care of yourself and reaching forth to live your best life.

How to let go of clutter in your home
Set aside a specific amount of time for decluttering, and stick to it.

It takes time to clean and organize your space. It takes more than five minutes to do a large decluttering task. Instead, I prefer to allocate at least an hour to each decluttering endeavor.

If you're ready to devote significant time to organizing your home, put a date in your calendar. To spread it out over several weekends or days off, you might need to break it up into smaller parts.

Do not keep more than one year's worth of belongings.
Remembering that "maybe I'll use this stuff later" is a bad habit. Nope! You can't think like a packrat if you want to maintain your house clutter-free. If possible, get rid of or donate whatever you haven't used in the last year.

Make sure there aren't any dupes.
It's time to get rid of anything you have multiples of (unless it's a storage item like a lightbulb or battery). It's easy to lose track

of what we already own, resulting in a need to replenish our supplies. We occasionally make improvements while retaining a less-than-ideal or inferior product.

This is particularly pertinent to your decluttering efforts when it comes to cleaning and arranging your closets and drawers. It isn't necessary to own a total of five white sweaters, I assure you. Sort your multiples, such as slacks, shirts, and other clothing and accessories. Gather all the items that fit and are in good condition. The best should be maintained, while the rest should be given away or thrown away.

Make a designated area for items that you want to keep.
Nothing can exist without a home. EVERYTHING. Even if it's going to be stored away. Organizing your drawers with clever container solutions will help you make the most of your available storage space. Organize and store what you want to keep in creative ways. My preferred method of helping me arrange items in my cupboards is to utilize aesthetically pleasing boxes, trays, and even old Kleenex boxes (and to organize tough areas, like underneath the sink). Get creative if you're going to keep it.

When decluttering, what should you do if you come across items that don't fit in the designated drawer or container? The next step is for you to go back to is step 2.

Make the most of the storage space provided by your furniture.
The fourth step is to make the most of these spaces. Storage desks, under-bed storage, and plain bookcases are all possibilities. With proper storage containers, you'll be amazed at how much extra space is available in these locations.

Tucking items into spots inside your existing furniture is a great way to hide them. Several storage containers are specifically built for weird, underutilized places like the back of your bed, between refrigerator shelves, or in the vertical space of your garage.

Each item should have its label.
What is it about Pinterest's organizing concepts that makes them so appealing? It's because of their straightforward labeling. When you view the finished product neatly placed in your storage locations, you'll recognize that the time spent labeling was well worth it.

The invention of a label maker is a wonderful triumph! An added visual element is created by labeling a stack of boxes. No matter how dark it is, you can still figure out what's in a box or behind a dark cabinet. You won't have to sift through your neatly organized space later to find something you've forgotten about, which will prevent it from being disorganized. It's easy to pinpoint its location.

Reduce paper clutter by digitizing your mementos.
Do you have a lot of pictures? I'm sure I do! It is, however, possible to store all of them on our laptops, which is a great benefit (or cloud storage). It may be difficult to part with sentimental items if you're new to digital storage, but once you see how much paper clutter is minimized, you'll be persuaded to make the switch.

I save my images on both my PC and in the cloud to keep my images safe. If one storage method fails, I know they'll be secure in the other. I organize them by year on my PC, then make a subfolder for each activity and date. To sort, I just drag & drop the photographs into the appropriate folders. I copy the identical folders to the cloud after the photographs are safely arranged. Done!

Divide your remaining items into three piles.
After you've pared down your belongings, labeled, and assigned a place for each item you want to keep, you'll likely be left with a significant mound of trash. Trash, sell and donate the items in your "don't keep" piles.

To begin, determine whether or not each thing is marketable. Consider selling items on Craigslist or eBay if you no longer need them. Remember to check out your local secondhand and consignment shops. It's a good idea to sell some of your belongings, and you may even make some extra money!

If you can't sell anything that's in good condition, give it away for the remainder of your belongings. In addition to clothing, dishes, and toys, Goodwill and the Salvation Army frequently accept donations. Remember that if you don't sell or donate the item within a week, it's time to throw it away. Trash bags should not be saved. Get rid of it and move on.

Make it a point to return all artifacts to their original position after use.
Decluttering your home is a good place to start. Keeping your house clean and clutter-free can be a real challenge. Change your mindset and include structure in your daily routine to become more efficient. After using an item, make it a point to return it to the store.

Return it if it previously lived there. We've all done it because we've grown tired of doing the same things over and over again. I'm one of the most horrendously awful wrongdoers regarding reserving merchandise close to the front entry. If you come into my house, you'll most likely see a stack of my shoes. When I come in, I take them off and never return to put them away. I promise I'm doing something about it!

Make another decluttering session a priority.
Unfortunately, this is not a one-time opportunity. Clutter needs to be dealt with at least once every three to six months if you want to avoid it getting out of hand again. It'll be a regular procedure, and you'll need to schedule time for it and make it a priority on your calendar.

But I'm confident you'll succeed! You could even enlist the support of your girlfriends and turn it into a wine night. Friendship is one of the most powerful motivators for letting go of things you don't need.

How to Declutter Your Home, Room by Room
Even if you're trying to downsize or simplify your life, decluttering your entire home is a huge undertaking. The greatest method to make decluttering simpler is to do it in phases. Concentrate on one room, one area, or even one zone inside a room (like your kitchen cupboards), and finish the work before going on to the next. As you achieve tangible accomplishments at each level, you will gain confidence.

There are no expensive instruments required for decluttering your home; however, you will need five baskets or containers for these five purposes:

Put Away: All items that have found their way into an undesignated storage space will be placed in this container. A coffee cup in the bathroom or a sweater in the kitchen could serve as examples of clutter. In other words, everything here will be put back exactly where it belongs.

Recycle: Paper, plastic, and glass are all recyclable in this bin.

Store them in this container if you have a favorite pair of shoes that you don't want to get dirty.

Garbage: Set aside one basket for goods to be placed in the household trash.

Donate: Set aside a bin for goods you may give to a nonprofit organization or a friend. These should be products that you can envision someone else desiring or needing.

You can utilize containers, baskets, or even cardboard boxes for this activity. As you declutter, bring these containers into each room or keep them in a central location in your home while you work. The crucial thing is that you don't look for containers when decluttering; instead, prepare the bins ahead of time.

Here are some of the finest ways to declutter each area in your house using these five containers.

The Bathroom

Begin by going through your medicine cabinet. Remove everything from the room and toss out expired prescriptions, cosmetics, or skincare items. Put everything you're retaining back into the cabinet right away, with the products you use the most kept at eye level.

After that, go through any cabinet drawers. Remove everything and make a fast assessment of what you'll retain and what you'll throw. Put the goods you'll keep back into their drawers, placing the items you use the most often at the top.

Begin by taking a shower or bath, then follow the same procedure. Finally, clean up the space beneath your sink of any accumulated debris.

Finally, everything that doesn't have a place may be swiftly divided into the five baskets or containers you've set aside.

The Bedroom

Make your bed first. It's difficult to make any headway decluttering a bedroom while you're staring at an unmade bed.

Begin with your nightstands, removing everything that doesn't belong, and placing it in the Put-Away bucket. Books you've previously done reading, broken eyeglasses, pencils and paper, and mail are all examples of this. Throw out or discard anything you don't use, such as empty tissue boxes, dried pencils, or dead chargers.

Assemble the tops of your dressers, chests, and bureaus in the same way. Pay special attention to any strewn-about garments. Everything that needs to be folded or hung goes into the Put-Away bucket. Spread it out on your bed if you're worried about wrinkles.

Go through each bureau one by one, drawer by drawer. Everything in the room should be taken out. Your donation bag or box should be full of stuff you no longer need. Maintainable clothing should be folded and stored.

The best place to begin is on a vanity table or desk in your bedroom. The Put-Away container is a better option than pushing items back into drawers. Throw away or recycle anything you haven't used in the last six months.

All of the items must be returned to their original positions. Folded or hung, every piece of clothing can be stored.

Closet and Clothing

Okay, take a deep breath. It's past time to clean up your closet. The simplest approach to clearing a wardrobe is to sort your clothes by category. Start with shoes, then boots, dresses, jeans, and so on.

When looking at your complete denim collection, it's much easier to determine whether to retain or dump a pair of jeans. So start picking out various clothing and deciding what you'll retain and throw.

You'll have four heaps to deal with once you've gone through each category of clothing:

Anything that was just in the improper place should be put away. Put a pair of socks in your dresser if you have any in your closet.

Place any filthy clothes in the hamper or take them to the washing room.

Any items that require repair should be taken to a tailor or dry cleaning.

Take your garments to a donation center or a consignment shop to get rid of them (either online or a brick and mortar outlet).

The Entryway, Mudroom, and Foyer

Although you may not have a typical mudroom or foyer, you have an entranceway. Decluttering an entryway daily, no matter how modest, is the greatest approach to make it more practical.

Begin with any existing desks, consoles, or side tables in your entryway. Remove the contents of each drawer and make a rapid judgment whether to throw or retain each thing. Also, inspect the tops of each desk or console. Do you have a place to keep your keys and other valuables? Check that everything is in working order and that it isn't overly crowded.

Start with shoes and boots, then coats, and finally accessories in the hall closet, just like you would in any other closet.

Another location collects a lot of debris from other rooms in the foyer. Spend some time putting things away from other rooms that have found their way to the entrance.

The Kitchen

Cooking, dining, and socializing are all activities in the kitchen, so keeping it clutter-free might be difficult. A vast array of items fill the kitchen as a result. It's possible to declutter your kitchen by going through each section one at a time (such as cutting boards, glassware, cutlery, or bakeware).

This process begins with meticulously sanitizing and evaluating each site, then relocating everything to its rightful placement. Start with your pantry and top cabinets when it comes to organizing them. Work your way to the bottom cupboards, drawers, and the kitchen sink's basin.

Pay close attention to the numbers on your counters, and you'll be OK. Remove as many items as possible from the countertops and store them. Only keep products on your counters that you use daily.

Finally, take your Put Away bin and return any items that don't belong in the kitchen to their proper storage location elsewhere in the home.

The Living Room

One of the most difficult areas in your house to maintain clean regularly is the living room. For this reason, most living rooms lack sufficient storage space. Except for a few bookcases and a television stand, you'll have little to hide. The important thing is to:

Make permanent storage arrangements for objects like remote controls, periodicals, and books often utilized.

Regularly declutter this area.
Start with bookcases, consoles, and side tables. After that, move on to the television stand and coffee table. Empty them, inspect the contents, and restore them to their respective storage locations. Books should be put away; paper clutter, such as mail, should be reduced; remote controls should be returned to their correct locations; blankets should be folded; and so on.

Now it's time to talk about electronics. Remove everything from your television or home theater system that isn't linked to it. Are you making use of it? Is it effective? Chargers, devices, and gaming equipment should all be kept close to where you use them.

Finally, the toys. Each toy should be examined for signs of wear and tear. Do you know if it's still up and running? Are your kids still using it? Each toy is imperative to be reused or stored in a safe place.

Take out your Put Away container and put anything that belongs in another room back where it belongs.

HELPING YOURSELF LET GO OF A LOVED ONE

It's never easy to let go of someone you care about.

When we finally acknowledge that it's time to say goodbye, it's as if we're saying goodbye to a significant part of ourselves.

Every funny memory, inside joke, and snapshot - letting go of your spouse means letting go of everything you've had together, and that's a decision we often don't want to make.

However, there are instances when you just have to go inside yourself and realize that it's finished, it's done, and it's time to move on.

Separate Yourself

Separating oneself from the person you love entails more than simply placing physical distance between you. Separation refers to the mental and emotional distance between you and that individual.

Being in love makes you feel as if your energies are aligned, as if you truly understand what the other person is going through and can empathize with them better than anyone else.

Disassociation is the first step in letting go. Remind yourself that this is your trip and no one else's.

Consider yourself as a separate person from your now-ex-desires partner's and feelings.

Know Your Self-Worth

I understand.

This piece of advice will come out as obvious and cliched. It will, nevertheless, be quite beneficial.

To let go of someone you care about, you must first focus on the essential connection you will ever have: your relationship with yourself.

A breakup is a negative reflection on our self-worth for many people.

Because breaking up is about losing the person you believed you were while with them, not just the person you loved.

Nevertheless, it is difficult to adore oneself. We're taught from an early age that pleasure comes from the outside, from finding the "ideal person." This is a dangerous misconception.

Declare Your "Whys"

Moving ahead is a self-imposed task, and like all missions, you'll need a clear purpose to keep you motivated to complete it.

It's difficult to let go of someone you care about.

When it comes to love, there are a million methods to persuade yourself to go back and stay with that person, regardless of how hopeless or difficult it is.

As a result, you must put your desire to move forward into easy, repeated terms, such as I'm moving on because I don't believe my spouse and I have the same life objectives.

Rather than squander time hoping for someone who will never return my affections, I'm moving on.

Making a clear statement of why you want to move forward can help you keep on course and concentrate on completing your journey.

Focus on yourself

Being separated from the person you love might make you feel lost. You have the impression that a piece of yourself is missing. That is why it is critical to devote time to yourself and reconnect with your emotions and sensations.

Even if you aren't in the mood.

Stop Fantasizing

Distancing oneself from the person you love entails ceasing to visualize yourself with them.

Any type of imagining involving this person has to end, whether it's benign musings about your prospective future together or erotic dreams now and again.

To truly let go of someone, you must allow yourself the time and space to unlearn and become unfamiliar with them.

If they're on your mind all the time, you'll be inclined to analyze the scenario and imagine the two of you together.

Accept Your Grief

Leaving another person behind, no matter how amicable your split is, is still difficult. Accept your pain, but don't let it fuel thoughts of regret and self-pity.

Don't try to hide your feelings or act as if they don't exist. Accepting your sentiments for what they are, unfettered by your now-ex-view, a partner is a vital element of committing to yourself.

Whatever sentiments or convictions you have about the relationship or circumstance, know that you may express them now without fear of being judged.

Make Plans

To progress, you must take measures that will truly propel you forward.

This entails devoting time and effort to activities and people that will enrich your life.

Having plans will spark your enthusiasm, curiosity, and interest in the world, bringing you new experiences that will fill the gap in your life.

Use this opportunity to develop as a person in general, not just as a future lover. Consider taking up a new pastime or reconnecting with pals you haven't seen in a while.

The goal of this phase is to keep you so occupied that your life no longer resembles the one you had with your partner. Consider it as a way to conclude a prior chapter and begin a new one.

Reconnect with your values

Taking pride in who you are is an important step toward self-sufficiency. It's challenging to rethink who you are once a relationship ends.

This is a good moment to think about your most fundamental values. Examine your beliefs and determine whether you hold them firmly or are influenced by them.

By dismantling your present ideals, you may find what you truly believe in, like doing, and stand for without the influence of others.

Getting a notepad and writing down your ideas and feelings is one of the finest methods to achieve this.

Writing allows your mind to relax and organize the data in your thoughts.

Remember that expressing, understanding, and delving deeply into your various feelings is an important aspect of getting over someone you love.

Journaling allows you to express your emotions in a secure setting. Nobody will read what you've written.

You might be enraged or depressed. Let out whatever it is you're feeling. Feelings should be processed.

Consider the following three questions if you're unsure where to begin:

- What›s going on inside of me?
- Do you know what you›re doing?
- What aspects of my life am I hoping to improve?

If you're having trouble understanding your feelings, try asking yourself these questions.

It's liberating to realize that you're in charge of your destiny. To take control of your life and lead it in the direction you desire, you don't need to rely on anyone else.

Try to figure out your ideal partner's characteristics.
To get over someone you care about, you must examine the relationship and determine the pros and cons.

Whatever the cause of the breakup, it's critical that you absorb your lessons to have a good future relationship.

Are you living up to your full potential? (Be truthful.) Take this 3-minute quiz to see what you need to do to attain your best potential.

And, for women, I believe that learning about what motivates men in relationships is the greatest approach to assure future success.

Because guys have a different perspective on the world than you do and are motivated by different things when it comes to love.

Men are born with an innate longing for something "higher" than love or sex. It's why guys who appear to have the "ideal girlfriend" are unsatisfied and are always looking for something else — or, worse, someone else.

Simply put, males have a biological need to feel wanted, significant, and capable of providing for the woman they love.

Make Peace With The Past
It's difficult to move forward when things are holding you back.

Perhaps you feel guilty for not being the greatest partner you might have been or for wishing to quit the relationship.

Remind yourself that, despite your sentiments of love, desire, and happiness, there is a part of you that wants to let go of this person and be alone.

Regardless of how much you care about them, a stronger, wiser part of you understands it's time to go on.

Consider anything is holding you back — guilt, rage, unsolved difficulties, unjust accusations, unrequited love – to be resolved.

Remember, you're not trying to heal the relationship; you're ready to go ahead on your own, so dwelling on previous mistakes or lost opportunities is pointless.

What Was It Like to Be a Single Person?

It might be difficult to imagine a future without another person in your life. So it's vital to reflect on the moments before the relationship to re-calibrate your self-organization.

You can gain strength from knowing that there was a period when you were completely self-sufficient, joyful, and capable without the presence of another person in your life.

It's simpler to accept a new chapter in your tale if you think of the breakup as just another incident in your life.

Time to Move Forward and Create a New Life

Here are some self-evaluation questions to consider:

Is it better to be surrounded by friends and family or alone?

What new things can I do to enhance myself and enrich my life?

What type of person do I want to be now that I've learned what I've learned from my past relationship?

It's time to do things that will genuinely assist you to go forward after you've rebuilt your identity and taken joy in who you are.

It might be as easy as reconnecting with old acquaintances or keeping a notebook to chronicle your emotions.

There are a variety of steps you may take to get started. It's all about finding purpose in life in the end.

Being in a relationship isn't the only way to have a sense of purpose. Romantic connections provide us with a sense of belonging, which is why they hold so much value for us.

Our feeling of kinship was never in dispute when we were all hunter-gatherers.

We were members of a tribe, residents of the area, and contributors to the ecology. That has now changed.

It's up to us to find our tribe. Many people live far away from or are alienated from their families.

We encounter several sets of friends throughout our life and must choose which ones we truly connect with.

More of us will never have children, and those who do will do so considerably later in life than our parents and grandparents did.

That is why a connection can provide us with a sense of belonging and significance. Our companion is someone with whom we can travel the globe.

A healthy relationship may help us feel grounded while also strengthening us to progress. On the other hand, a relationship may rip our feeling of purpose and belonging apart.

We will be unable to interact with the world authentically if we are in a relationship that seems inappropriate.

Investing most of your energy with somebody you don't cherish and who doesn't genuinely adore you contrarily affects your ability to interface with others.

Viktor Frankl, a former concentration camp inmate during WWII, published the book Man's Search for Meaning.

He talked about how even individuals in the most difficult of situations seek connection and belonging.

Individuals on the edge of being hungry would give up their last piece of bread and soothe others. Meaning is at the root of everything.

"Our greatest freedom is the ability to choose our attitude," says one of Frankl's most famous phrases.

That's an important thing to keep in mind following a breakup. Breakups are tumultuous and difficult to manage.

We feel that our emotions are racing ahead of us and that there is nothing we can do to stop them.

We worry that our life will not be what we expected. Frankl would argue that we should seek significance differently by changing our perspective.

Establish A Morning And Night Routine

Why It's Beneficial: It's tough to go back to normal after a breakup, which is why having a routine is crucial.

It will make every day more interesting if you have something to look forward to when you wake up and go home from work and school.

Perhaps you can start a new skincare routine or make sure you're eating nutritious dinners.

It doesn't matter what you do with your free time.

Its goal is to provide a much-needed incentive to wake up every day and go on by laying out a clear morning and evening schedule.

How To Make This Happen:
Incorporate self-care into your morning and nighttime routines to make them more pleasurable.

Within two weeks of the breakup, try to go back into your routine as much as possible. After you start feeling better, you may be more flexible with your schedule.

For weekends and weekdays, experiment with alternative regimens. On weekday mornings, you might want to start your day with a podcast, and on weekends, you might want to enjoy brunch with friends first thing in the morning.

Without Your Partner, Letting Go: Finding Positivity, Growth, and Opportunity in Yourself Instead of seeing this as letting go of someone and losing a piece of yourself, turn the circumstance around and see it as an opportunity to develop who you are as an individual.

Your trip didn't start with that one person, and it's unlikely to end there.

Remind yourself of your potential before you fell in love, as well as the many more opportunities you'll have once you've moved on.

Let it Go

close your eyes, clear your heart, let it go

Rumination

If you're like most individuals, you've experienced ruminating about a distressing event that occurred throughout your day. Whatever it was that hit you in the gut, whatever it was that made you wish you'd said, whatever it was that's been repeating over and over in your head without providing any clarity, there's a good chance it was someone else.

Rumination happens when these ideas get more dark and brooding. This essay's goal is to clarify what rumination is and the possible negative consequences. It also addresses how to avoid concentrating on one's self-defeating thoughts.

What Is Rumination?

Rumination is characterized by recurrent, excessive ideas that obstruct other sorts of thinking. This thinking is frequent in persons with illnesses like generalized anxiety disorder and obsessive-compulsive disorder. Still, it is also typical in people who do not have a diagnosable problem from time to time.

Rumination is both stressful and frequent in that it takes a challenging circumstance and multiplies the tension and the importance of the issue in our thoughts.

Rumination is made up of two components: contemplation and brooding.

Rumination with reflection: The reflection element can be beneficial since reflecting on a problem might lead to a solution. Additionally, thinking about specific occurrences might aid in processing powerful emotions related to the problem.

In general, rumination and brooding have been linked to less proactive activity and a more negative mood.

Rumination also focuses on the sense of powerlessness that comes with not changing what has already occurred. We may not recreate the circumstance in the future and reply with the ideal retort, answer, or solution, making us feel helpless and agitated.

Finally, seeing how much time and energy we spent pondering the topic might lead to even more aggravation.

Co-rumination, which involves rehashing an issue with friends until you've exhausted all options, increases tension for both parties after it has passed the point of being useful.

As such, assuming you end up rehashing occasions in your mind, waiting on the unfairness, all things considered, and contemplating how you ought to have said or treated following up on it, you're expanding your feelings of anxiety. You're probably also feeling some of the negative consequences of ruminating.

Causes of Rumination

So, why do people get so worked up over things? Different people tend to obsess over different topics for different reasons, and some people appear to be more prone to it than others.

Some individuals repeat rehearsing a circumstance they can't seem to understand or accept because they seek to make sense of it. Others desire confirmation that they were correct (especially if they feel unconscious that they were wrong).

Some individuals attempt to address the problem or prevent such events in the future but cannot do so. On the other hand, others may want to be heard and affirmed or to feel justified in absolving themselves of blame.

A variety of circumstances can trigger rumination. People occasionally make the error of thinking that they can obtain control of a situation by repeatedly going over an occurrence or repeating particular sentiments.

This form of thinking is something that most individuals do from time to time. You may find yourself overthinking a stressful occasion in the days leading up to it. You can reflect on everything you wish you had done differently when a relationship ends.

In most circumstances, these ruminating thoughts go away as other issues take precedence in your mind. These thoughts may be a symptom of a mental health problem if they are persistent and feel uncontrollable.

Rumination can be a sign of several mental health problems. The following are some of the conditions linked to ruminating thoughts:

- Depression
- Generalized anxiety disorder (GAD)
- Obsessive-compulsive disorder (OCD)
- Phobias
- Post-traumatic stress disorder (PTSD)

The Negative Effects of Rumination

Rumination begins innocently enough: your mind attempts to make sense of an unpleasant circumstance and move on. However, it might trap you in a never-ending cycle of aggravation and tension. When you're coping with long-term difficulties in your relationships, excessive ruminating can cause chronic stress.

It's critical to learn how to recognize rumination before becoming engrossed in it and how to handle problems healthily.

Rumination has an oddly alluring quality to it, and it may easily capture your attention before you know you're worrying again. Rumination has various harmful impacts in addition to diverting your attention.

Stress

Several successful mindfulness books, like Jon Kabat-"There Zinn's You Are" and Eckhart Tolle's "The Power of Now" and "A New Earth, and Wherever You Go," have been hailed as good stress-relieving aids.

Because they demonstrate how to significantly minimize rumination, which contributes to a stressed state of mind, these books are so helpful at relieving stress.

Studies have shown rumination to increase cortisol levels, indicating a physiologic stress response.

Possessing a Negative Attitude.

Rumination, predictably, is supposed to have a negative effect by making people feel more gloomy and dissatisfied. This negative mindset has a whole new set of implications.

Less Proactive Behavior

While people may meditate to work through an issue and find a solution, research has found that excessive rumination is linked to less proactive activity, increased disengagement from problems, and a more negative state of mind. As a result, rumination might lead to a negative downward cycle.

Self-Sabotage

Rumination has been connected to harmful coping strategies such as binge eating studies. Self-destructive coping strategies can increase stress levels, sustaining a negative and destructive cycle.

Hypertension

There's also a correlation between meditating and high blood pressure. Rumination can lengthen the stress response, increasing the harmful effects of stress on the heart. Because of the health hazards associated with hypertension, it's vital to avoid ruminating and develop appropriate stress management and coping skills.

Recap

Rumination has many negative health effects, including increased stress, self-sabotage, and reduced good thoughts and activities. It can also hurt your physical health, increasing your risk of hypertension.

Overcoming Rumination

While knowing why you're contemplating might help you develop coping mechanisms, it's frequently more important to figure out quitting. Here are some suggestions for catching yourself and refocusing.

Establish a Time Limit

It can be beneficial to seek support and affirmation from friends. Still, too much talk about other people's wrongdoings can create a negative and gossipy dynamic in your relationships, reinforcing the situation's dissatisfaction rather than seeking answers and closure.

Keep an Open Mind

Several therapists have indicated that what genuinely bothers us about others reflects what we don't accept in ourselves.

Can you rely on a comparable experience in yourself to help you better grasp the other person's perspective and the reasons for what they did when you think about what made you angry?

Can you relate with them, even if you don't agree with them? The loving-kindness meditation may be an excellent tool for forgiving and letting go, as well as a powerful antidote to ruminating.

Create Boundaries

"The first time, shame on you; the second time, shame on me," as the saying goes. It wonderfully illustrates responsibility and the need to set limits. It helps you learn something new about yourself and the other person with each meeting, allowing you to influence the way things proceed in the future.

Examine what happened through the lens of change, not to blame the other person for your suffering, but to find solutions that will avoid the same thing from happening again. Where might you have said no sooner or protected yourself better in the future? Come from a position of strength and understanding rather than being offended or angry.

You can modify your habitual thought patterns with practice, and this is a great case where such a shift might revolutionize your stress experience. It won't happen overnight, but you'll quickly stop obsessing over things and feel less emotional tension as a consequence.

Reduce your stress levels by keeping your mind on the task at hand.

CONCLUSION

When our lives get cluttered with emotions, we have less room for important things like our personal development and fulfillment. Finding happiness frequently entails learning to see past all of the surface, self-defeating behaviors, and habits to get to the heart of the problem.

Begin with decluttering your life and getting rid of the stuff you don't need. Cut out the activities, hobbies, and relationships that make you unhappy; go through your belongings and let go of the non-essential items and people that deplete you. Say "no" more frequently and advocate for your needs. Pursue your happiness and pare down your buddy list, removing those that cause you more grief than they help. Be present and begin to feel at ease in the actual world, free from the constant distractions of all the empty and worthless things you've clung to. By measuring your emotional temperature regularly, you may begin to sit with your feelings and become comfortable with them. We clog up our lives (more often than not) because we are afraid to face our emotions. Stop avoiding who you are and what you truly desire and master the art of letting go of things and people that no longer serve you.

Refusing to let go will not bring someone you care about back into your life. Holding on just exacerbates your mental and physical situation, preventing you from completely appreciating life. Accept that living in the now is the best way to live and that uncertainty, when viewed correctly, may be beautiful.

Face what has occurred, realize that you can't alter it, and moving on are the keys to letting go of someone you love. Better possibilities will come themselves once you've been ready to move on and appreciate the progress that came from the connection. You'll have mastered the art of letting go of someone you care about, and you'll be ready to start crafting your new tale.

Do Not Go Yet; One Last Thing To Do

If you enjoyed this book or found it useful, I'd be very grateful if you'd post a short review on Amazon. Your support does make a difference, and I read all the reviews personally so I can get your feedback and make this book even better.

Thanks again for your support!

If you enjoyed this title and would like to read about other topics that have changed my life, please check out my new books on Amazon or my website: www.my-mindguide.com.

Also, let's stay connected on social media. Please drop a line on Facebook or Instagram, and stay tuned for updates! You're welcome to share your thoughts with me directly as well: gassner@my-mindguide.com. In return, I'll send you a gorgeous infographic that you can cut out and frame.

Also, please leave a review on Amazon, as this will help me to reach an even broader audience. Thank you so much for your time, insight, and undying hunger for knowledge!

I want to say thank you to all of my colleagues, clients, friends, and family members, who have all contributed to what I am now.

I also want to say thank you to Gabriel Palacios, the king of hypnotherapy and a Swiss bestseller author who taught this old fox new tricks, letting me deep-dive into the mystery of hypnotherapy. I learned so much along the journey that I'm now a certified master-hypnosis coach and conversation coach myself!

Furthermore, I want to say thank you to the fantastic teachers of SAMYANA/Bali who trained me to become a certified yoga and meditation teacher.

Last but not least, I give a special thanks to my master-teacher Eckhard Wunderle, who's close to a saint to me. He introduced me to the world of meditation and let me discover all the wonders it has to offer. I couldn't be more proud about having received my certification as a meditation teacher from directly from him at the Institut für Spirituelle Psychologie.

Peace, love, and happiness to all of you—till next time!

Authors portrait

Kurt Friedrich Gassner has worn many hats throughout his lifetime, including but not limited to serial entrepreneur, Creative Director, Meditation Teacher, Licensed Hypnotherapist, and more recently, self-improvement author. Leveraging his treasure trove of experiences and in-depth knowledge of psychology, he provides his readers with the tools they need to unlock their infinite potential.

As a prolific self-help writer, Kurt has authored the following books: *The Art of Forgiveness*, *Lie or Die*, *Soul-Match*, *Can You Inherit a Poisoned Mind?* and *The Power of Poverty*. He also authored a best-selling children's book in German-speaking countries and has over 20 books underway.

When it comes to enduring success, Kurt understands that financial prosperity isn't the only aspect one should strive for. He may be a self-made millionaire, but what really transformed his life is mastering his unconscious mind. Perseverance, personal power, self-awareness, and learning from past mistakes have all been key ingredients to bringing his dreams to fruition—and he strives to impart that wisdom onto others through his writing.

During his spare time, Kurt Friedrich Gassner is either traveling across the globe, golfing, biking in the Alps, hiking, or spending quality time with his loved ones. For the last 37 years, he has been happily married and he is the father of two successful children. Presently, he resides in both Munich, Germany, and Kirchberg, Austria.

OTHER BOOKS BY THE AUTHOR

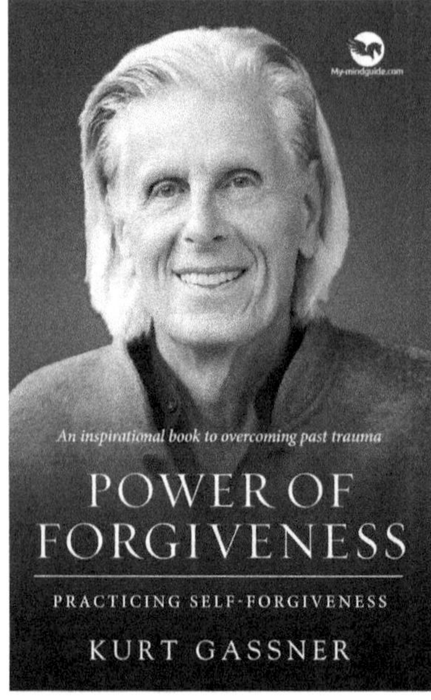

BÜCHER VOM AUTOR IN DEUTSCHER AUSGABE

OTHER BOOKS BY THE AUTHOR

OTHER BOOKS BY THE AUTHOR

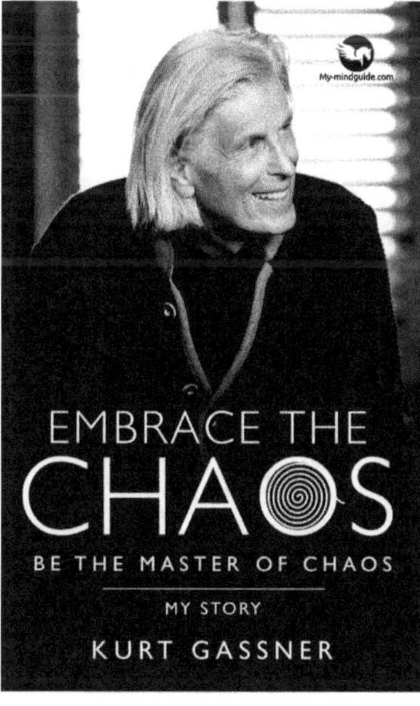

TRUE STORIES AND MANAGEMENT LESSONS FOR OUR TOUGH CHANGING TIMES

KURT GASSNER

ECKO

WEGEN ERFOLG GEFEUERT

Eine wahre Geschichte über das Scheitern in Unternehmen und was junge Führungskräfte aus einer Fehlerkultur lernen können.

KURT GASSNER

My-mindguide.com

Unlocking The Healing Power of Pets

What Pets Can Tell You About Your Soul

KURT GASSNER

My-mindguide.com

Heilkraft Unserer Lieblinge

Was Haustiere über Ihre Seele verraten können

KURT GASSNER

My-mindguide.com
THE
BLISS OF
STRUGGLE
WINNING STRATEGIES
FOR DEMANDING TIMES
KURT GASSNER

My-mindguide.com
STARK
DURCH
„STRUGGLES"
DAS IDEALE MINDSET,
UM KRISEN ZU MEISTERN
KURT GASSNER

My-mindguide.com
LIE LYING
& LIAR
A LIE HAS NO LEGS BUT IT HAS WINGS
KURT GASSNER

My-mindguide.com
LÜGE LÜGEN
& LÜGNER
EINE LÜGE HAT KEINE BEINE, ABER SIE HAT FLÜGEL
KURT GASSNER

BORN
in the
COLD
Liebe und Aufmerksamkeit in der Wachstumsphase eines Kindes
KURT GASSNER

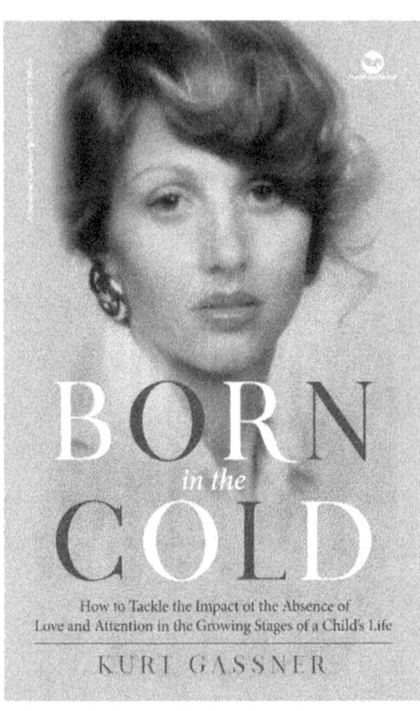
BORN
in the
COLD
How to Tackle the Impact of the Absence of
Love and Attention in the Growing Stages of a Child's Life
KURT GASSNER

SOPHIAS WUNDERWELT
10 ERZÄHLUNGEN
KURT GASSNER

SOPHIA'S WONDERWORLD
10 TALES
KURT GASSNER

BESTSELLING AUTHOR OF
The Art Of
FORGIVNESS
AMAZON
#1
BESTSELLER
My-mindguide.com
A practical guide for
self healing and
overcome past traumas
The Art Of
FORGIVNES
KURT GASSNER
The Art Of
FORGIVNESS
KURT GASSNER

See me also on Wikipedia

https://en.wikipedia.org/wiki/Kurt_Gassner

www.ingramcontent.com/pod-product-compliance
Lightning Source LLC
LaVergne TN
LVHW050540160826
845677LV00011B/2116

* 9 7 8 3 9 8 7 9 3 0 1 6 4 *